EDUARDO DE FILIPPO

INNER
VOICES

ENGLISH VERSION BY

N.F. SIMPSON

AMBER LANE PRESS

All rights whatsoever in this play are strictly reserved and
application for performance, etc. should be made before
rehearsal to:

Dr Jan van Loewen Ltd
21 Kingly Street
London W1R 5LB

Le voci di dentro was first
published in 1951 by Giulio
Einaudi, Turin, Italy.

This edition first published in 1983 by
Amber Lane Press Ltd
9 Middle Way
Oxford OX2 7LH

Printed in Great Britain by
Cotswold Press Ltd, Oxford

ISBN 0 906399 45 9

CHARACTERS

THE CIMMARUTA FAMILY

PASQUALE	50	
MATHILDE	40's	Pasquale's wife
LUIGI	20	Son
ELVIRA	18	Daughter
ROSA	55	Pasquale's sister
MARIA	20's	Maid

THE SAPORITO FAMILY

ALBERTO	50	
CARLO	40's	Alberto's brother
ZI NICOLA	82	Their uncle

MICHELE	Hall Porter
ANIELLO AMITRANO	A neighbour
TERESA AMITRANO	Aniello's wife
CAPA D'ANGELO	A secondhand furniture dealer

LIEUTENANT and CARABINIERI

The play is set in Naples in 1948.

This English version of *Inner Voices* was first presented in the Lyttleton Theatre at the National Theatre, London on 16 June 1983. It was directed by Mike Ockrent, with the following cast:

ALBERTO	Ralph Richardson
CARLO	Michael Bryant
ZI NICOLA	Daniel Thorndike
ROSA	Avril Elgar
MARIA	Diane Bull
MATHILDE	Marjorie Yates
PASQUALE	Robert Stephens
LUIGI	Stephen Hattersley
ELVIRA	Catherine Hall
MICHELE	Glenn Williams
LIEUTENANT	Nicholas Selby
CAPA D'ANGELO	David Sterne
TERESA AMITRANO	Mary Macleod
ANIELLO AMITRANO	John Dallimore
CARABINIERI	Charles Baillie, Colin Haigh, Ian Hurley, Richard Perkins, Stag Theodore

INTRODUCTION

Inner Voices was written and first performed in Naples in 1948, with the author playing the part of Alberto Saporito. Both time and place are important because the play is about two neighbouring households in Naples and the effect on them of what they had lived through for the previous twenty years or so. There had been Fascist dictatorship, and war, and military occupation by both German 'allies' and British and American 'liberators'; and the poverty, which was and is a permanent feature of life in Naples, had become near-starvation. These were the conditions under which survival had come to mean abandoning scruples, lying low, placating authority, knowing what it paid you to know and what it paid you not to know. It meant saving your own skin at no matter whose expense, and it created a climate in which the informer came into his own. It afforded opportunities to pay off old scores and do down rivals; it gave ample scope to spite and malice, and full rein to envy and resentment. It bred fear and suspicion, and made for a society in which accusations, whether they have substance in them or not, are dangerous. Ordinary people might well, in such circumstances, lose their heads in a crisis, and be driven to absurd extremes. The spectacle of seemingly respectable people falling over themselves to avoid being implicated in a crime that had never been committed, and going to pieces in a panic-stricken orgy of mutual denunciation, is both comic and painful, like so much else of human experience. Solemn farce and knockabout tragedy become indistinguishable from one another as fear makes fools of us all, betraying us into behaviour and attitudes that are less than edifying and serve no purpose other than to diminish us. *Inner Voices* says all this, and says it better.

The play which follows is an English version of the Neapolitan original. It is not an adaptation. How then, to make the play accessible to an English-speaking audience without, in so doing, taking away from it its own flavour and quality, or giving it a falsifying emphasis which would make it into a different play from the one as written by Eduardo de Filippo? Neapolitan is to standard Italian (if there is such a thing) as Geordie or Scouse or Cockney might be to standard English, and, as such, is not always comprehensible outside Naples, even to Italians. Hopeless, though, to try for some regional equivalent in English because this would place the play somewhere other than in Naples, when its whole authenticity depends on its being firmly rooted in its time and place. What I settled for was a kind of uncoloured speech, articulate but without, so far as possible, intimations of class, region or period, and having its own cadences and rhythms, and such grace and formal elegance as I could give it. I wanted it to be in English without saying England; and I wanted the language, while having a life of its own, to be able to take on such colour as the actors would give it in performance. This was in itself, of course, a compromise, as all translation must be, but it seemed the least damaging of the various compromises open to me.

Much the same considerations determined the style of the acting and of the production as a whole. The possibility, indeed likelihood, that what we would have would be set in a kind of vaguely Italianate limbo, rather than in a genuinely authentic Naples, was obvious; but this, unavoidable in any English production of any Italian play, was, I think, a positive advantage in this one. The most one can hope for is to present what to an English audience is plausibly Italian, with nothing jarring or seeming obviously incongruous, or drawing attention to itself by necessarily unsuccessful attempts to *be* Italian. What this does is to put the play in the area that most of Shakespeare's plays inhabit for a modern audience, and many of them inhabited for a contemporary audience, where we can be both caught up in the action and at the same time distanced from it. This works for, rather than against, a play which is something of a parable, and is meant to be seen, if not instantly then certainly in retrospect, as a paradigm of human behaviour. In Naples, in 1948, *Inner Voices* may have been almost too near home for its wider significance to be apparent; but seen by an audience for whom these things are happening to other people somewhere else at some other time, and yet with recognisable, and unsettling, affinities with our own behaviour at all kinds of levels and in altogether different circumstances, it does far more than draw attention to a local phenomenon: it universalises it.

N.F. Simpson
August 1983

ACT ONE

A clean, shining kitchen in the Cimmarutas' apartment. There is a main door, right, leading to the front hall, and another smaller door, left, leading into the rest of the apartment.

ROSA *enters.*

ROSA: It's like moving heaven and earth getting you out of bed in the morning.

> [MARIA *enters, yawning. She has one shoe on and the other is in her hand. She sits down, sleepy and sluggish, and starts to put the other shoe on.*]

MARIA: I'm not properly awake yet! It takes me longer than other people to come round in the morning. You should never wake people up before they're ready. It's bad for you to be dragged out of bed when you're still half asleep.

ROSA: You're never anything else.

MARIA: I like to lie there for a bit and think about getting up. I feel terrible all day if I get up suddenly.

ROSA: I don't know what you're complaining about. You were in bed by nine o'clock...half past seven now...you've had ten and a half hours' sleep! How much sleep do you need?

MARIA: Some people need more than others. It's the way you're made. Besides which, you came and woke me in the middle. You should never break off in the middle of things...you're always telling me that.

ROSA: You've got sleeping sickness, my girl, that's what you've got.

MARIA: If I'd been born into some family with lots of money, do you know what? I'd have lovely soft beds everywhere. I'd have a bed in every room in the house, and then I could stretch out on it and sleep any time I wanted.

ROSA: Yes, well...you're here to earn your living, not lie in bed all day, and you'd better start learning to get up in the morning or you'll be earning it somewhere else.

MARIA: Oh, no, I wouldn't want to go anywhere else. I like it here. And they all stay in bed in the morning...you're the only one who doesn't. It'd be heaven here if it weren't for that.

ROSA: If you think I'm going to pack my bags and go away just to suit you...

MARIA: I didn't mean that. All I meant was that it'd be absolutely perfect if you didn't get up so early.

ROSA: Perhaps if I were anywhere but here, I might find it easier to sleep.

> [ROSA *has crossed to a table on which are some home-made candles and tablets of soap.*]

Instead, I do these. Do you know what...I don't think a single one of these has split... look at that one...they're beautifully firm, all of them...more than half of them split last time and had to be thrown away. The whole batch has turned out well. And so have the candles. These are like the ones we got before the war...Maria...

> [MARIA *has dropped off to sleep again.*]

...Maria!

MARIA: What...? What time is it?

ROSA: For goodness' sake, girl...will you wake up! You really will find yourself out on the street if you don't pull yourself together. I only have to mention it to don Pasquale.

MARIA: I hadn't finished! I keep telling you you woke me up in the middle!

ROSA: Finished or not, you've had all the sleep you're going to have. Come over here and look at these. Tell me what you think of them. Look at that...and that...and how beautifully firm and hard that one is...the whole batch has really come out well this time... and the candles.

MARIA: These are every bit as good as the ones you buy!

ROSA: We've got the war to thank for this. No one would have dreamt of making their own soap and candles before the war.

MARIA: You not only save money, but you've got the satisfaction as well.

ROSA: It shows what you can do if you really put your mind to something, my girl.

MARIA: You ought to open a shop.

ROSA: I've thought of it more than once. There's plenty of fat, provided you don't go throwing it away...daydreaming instead of keeping your mind on what you're doing. It's not as if I don't keep reminding you. *All* fat...oil, lard, dripping...anything that can be used...drain it off and put it to one side.

MARIA: Yes, I try to remember, but you forget.
[*The doorbell sounds.*]

ROSA: Go and see who that is.
[MARIA *goes out and comes back in with* MICHELE, *the hall porter. He is carrying a dish piled high with plums for eating, and a shopping bag bulging with groceries.*]

MICHELE: Good morning, donna Rosa.

ROSA: Good morning, Michele. Ah...you remembered them.

MICHELE: I'd have heard about it from your brother if I hadn't. The last thing don Pasquale said to

me last night was not to come without them.
It'd have been more than my life's worth to
forget them. I put the dish on a chair beside
the bed before I went to sleep to remind me
the minute I woke up. I thought, if I put that
there, I shall clap eyes on it first thing and say
to myself 'Ah…don Pasquale's plums!' What
do you think of them? Just right for eating,
aren't they? Nice and juicy. Plenty of flesh on
them. Not all stone and nothing else.

ROSA: No, they're fine. He'll be very pleased with
those.

MICHELE: And here's the rest.

ROSA: You've got everything…?

MICHELE: Yes. I've got your list here. I don't think I've
forgotten anything. My head's not as reliable
as it used to be. Struggling to make ends meet
and chasing round non-stop for the tenants
morning, noon and night…it's a wonder I
can think straight. So, if there is anything
missing, you'll have to blame the other tenants,
not me.

MARIA: What a horrible dream! It's just come back to
me. I was in the kitchen. I was sitting by the
window with my feet up washing some broccoli
and putting the tips in a bowl and this caterpillar dropped out. It was white all over, with
a black head, and it was just lying there looking at me. Then it spoke. Something about
having nowhere to live now because of me. So
I said 'What are you going to do, then?' and it
said 'Go to church, of course, and pray.' So I
said 'All right. I'll come with you. We can go
together.' So we went off and as we were walking it came on to rain, but the caterpillar had
an umbrella so that was all right, but when we
got to the church it was locked. I said 'Oh,
dear. What do we do now?' and the caterpillar

said 'Crawl under the door.' I said 'I can't crawl under the door. What do I do?' It said 'Wait where you are until someone comes with a key.' But I said 'It's raining!' So it said 'Here, take this,' and gave me its umbrella. I watched it crawl under the door and disappear, and then I put up the umbrella and started walking. As I was going along, I suddenly felt something dripping on to my head...just there...in the middle of my head...in exactly the same spot...so I thought 'Hallo, this umbrella's got a hole in it,' but when I looked up, it was perfectly all right, so where were the drops of water coming from? And then I thought 'The sooner I get back, the sooner I can put the umbrella down,' so I started walking faster. Then this drip, drip, drip started to feel as if it were burning a hole right through my head. It was like some sort of acid...eating its way through till it got to my tongue. Then it went right through to my stomach, and then my lungs, and then I heard a shout 'Don't burn me!' and I realised it was my heart that had jumped out of my body and was running away down the road. So I ran after it, shouting to it to stop. I said 'Come back, heart! How can I stay alive with no heart?' And then, just as I was turning into a side street, trying to get my breath and covered with perspiration running all down me, I came face to face with the caterpillar again. It was holding out a revolver and say- ing 'If you want to stay alive, take this and shoot that old tramp sitting over there on the pavement.' So I shot him, but...and this is the really grisly bit...I'd no sooner fired the gun than the tramp turned into a fountain and the caterpillar said 'What are you waiting for? If you're thirsty, why don't you have a drink?' So I did. And it wasn't water after all. It was blood. And I just went on drinking and drinking. Can you imagine a more horrible dream than that?

MICHELE: I wouldn't want to try. It's enough to turn your stomach over listening to that one.

ROSA: I don't know where dreams like that come from. I'm still getting over the one I had the other night. I'd forgotten all about it till this came up. I was in the kitchen.

MICHELE: In the middle of the night?

ROSA: I dreamt I was in the kitchen.

MICHELE: Oh, I see. We're going to hear your dream as well. Carry on.

ROSA: You'd just come in with the shopping, and I was putting it away and I'd got the meat on a plate and suddenly there was a voice. 'Aren't you going to see to me, then?' So I opened the kitchen door to see if there was anyone outside, and there was. It was a young lamb, all dressed up in a top hat, with a walking stick. As soon as it saw me, it took off its top hat and laid its walking stick down and came straight through the door into the kitchen and said 'Let's get on with it. I haven't got all day to waste.' So I put it on the table, took a knife, and cut its throat. Then I curled it round in the roasting tin with some potatoes and onions and put it in the oven. Next thing you know, we're all sitting round the table, with this delicious-looking roast in front of us. I was carving and serving. And then suddenly it wasn't a lamb any more. It was a baby. With fair curly hair. Someone'd got a foot and someone else had got a hand and someone else had got the head. And everyone was saying 'Mmmm, delicious! So tasty! Just right with this wine!' I was horrified. I'll never touch lamb again as long as I live. If it's ever put in front of me, I'll run screaming from the table.

MICHELE: Yes. I don't dream all that much myself. By the time I get to bed, I'm generally too tired for dreaming. It was different when I was younger. I had some really beautiful dreams then. I used to wake up in the morning on top of the world. It was a pleasure to go off to work after dreams like the ones I had then. They didn't seem like dreams at all. It was more like being in the theatre watching a play. When I woke up, all I wanted to do was to go back to sleep again to see how it ended.

MARIA: Oh, yes. So would I!

MICHELE: Everything was different then, though. Life was much more easygoing. People were more genuine. They said what they meant. There was nothing underhand. If you went to someone for advice, you knew you could rely on what he told you. Now you can't believe a word anyone says. As a result, you get dreams like Maria's, that leave a nasty taste in the mouth. Anyway, I can't stop here talking… I've got things to do. So, if you don't mind, you'll have to excuse me. [*to* MARIA] And my advice to you, young woman, is to get married and have a husband in bed beside you…then your dreams'll be all sunshine and roses.

MARIA: Does that go for donna Rosa too? She has bad dreams as well.

MICHELE: Certainly, if she wants to. There's no shortage of men who'd jump at the chance.

ROSA: That's enough of that, Michele, thank you.

MICHELE: I'll be off, then.

[*He goes.*]

ROSA: And you get a move on, too, Maria. We'll

have them all in here in a minute clamouring for coffee and wanting to know why it's not on the table.

MARIA: And we both know who the first one'll be.

ROSA: If you're talking about don Pasquale, I only wish he'd eat something when he does come. He's getting more and more haggard. I can see him wasting away in front of my eyes.

MARIA: It's because he worries too much, donna Rosa. It's all the things he keeps bottled up inside him instead of coming out with them.

ROSA: Things? What things? What do you know about it?

MARIA: Well...nothing...but everyone has things they worry about. It was only a remark.

ROSA: Yes, well, there's nothing on my brother's mind, so don't go jumping to conclusions on that score, my girl. [*She starts preparing coffee.*] And while I'm getting the coffee ready, you can be doing Elvira's zabaglione. I've put two eggs in the soup tureen on the dresser over there. You can use those. And remember to put a good four spoonfuls of sugar in.

[ROSA *lights the gas.*]

MARIA: She won't eat it. You know she won't. She doesn't like anything with eggs in.

ROSA: She'll have to like it. An eighteen-year-old girl out at work all day...especially the kind of work she does.

MARIA: I've never been all that sure what sort of work she does do.

ROSA: There's no reason why you should be. She's a shorthand typist, if you really want to know. With a legal firm. She has her notebook and she takes down what they're saying, and then she types it all out so that people can read it. I don't know how she understands it. She does one little squiggle like that...[*She traces a short-*

hand sign in the air with her finger.]…and it can stand for a whole paragraph. Something like that…[*another sign*]…might mean 'Dear Sir, The situation has turned out in the event to be considerably graver than we had reason to anticipate, and it would be our intention, therefore, to press for a firmer line to be taken…' And, doing that all day, she needs a good breakfast.

MARIA: It's very clever, isn't it? If it were me, I'd forget.

ROSA: It's good money, as well. She's well liked there, and she's getting on. Where are the breakfast rusks I put out for donna Mathilde?

MARIA: They're over there on the dresser.

ROSA: We shall want those on the table.

> [ROSA *gets them and puts them on the table.*]

MARIA: She's another one who can't sit still. Your sister-in-law. She's on the go all the time. It's all she can do, when she gets in at the end of the day, to collapse into a chair.

ROSA: Donna Mathilde has some very difficult people to deal with. You'd be all in. Probing into the future all the time for people. And if it's not the future, it's the past. 'Is so-and-so in America still alive?'…or 'The wife's pregnant again, Madame Omarbey, will it be a boy or a girl?' I keep telling her she's got to make them understand that all she can do is read the cards. She's not a clairvoyant.

MARIA: What I like is seeing your brother with his turban on, showing the customers in. 'Step this way, gentlemen, please.' [*She laughs.*] I think it's hilarious.

ROSA: He doesn't do it for fun! It's a matter of necessity. He wouldn't do it if he didn't have to. [*She smells burning.*] Now look what's happened.

You've made me burn the macaroni. That's through talking to you.

[ROSA *turns it over with a fork.*]

MARIA: If it's for your nephew, that's the way he likes it anyway. He prefers it burnt.

ROSA: He likes it crisp. He doesn't like it burnt.

MARIA: I don't know how anyone could eat macaroni first thing in the morning when they've only just got up. I couldn't.

ROSA: Luigi's a young man. He's got a young man's appetite. When you're that age, you go to bed hungry and wake up hungry. He needs a good breakfast.

MARIA: You've got quite a soft spot for Luigi, haven't you?

ROSA: He's my nephew, Maria. He's the only nephew I've got. And it's high time he was settling down. He's like the rest of them nowadays…they want to go their own way, and there's no talking to them.

[MATHILDE *enters in a dressing gown.*]

MATHILDE: Good morning.

MARIA: Good morning, donna Mathilde.

ROSA: I was just coming to wake you.

MATHILDE: I had the alarm on. I put it under the pillow, so that I could reach under and put it off without waking his excellency.

MARIA: He'll have heard it. It doesn't take much to wake don Pasquale. He's always got one ear cocked, anyway, even when he's asleep, in case you're up to something.

MATHILDE: If he has, that's his look-out. I've long since given up worrying about that.

ROSA: Have some coffee. It's almost ready.

MATHILDE: No. I'll try the dress on first.

MARIA: While you can. Once don Pasquale comes in here, that'll be that.

[ROSA *takes a dress of the sort a fortune-*

teller might wear from off a tailor's dummy. It still has the tacking stitches in it.]

ROSA: Here it is. I've done the alterations.

[MATHILDE *takes off her dressing gown. Underneath she has on a short, low-cut slip. She puts on the dress.*]

MATHILDE: Did you do the slit up the front?

ROSA: Yes. I've taken it right up to above the knee.

MATHILDE: But it's on the wrong side. It should be over this way...because when I sit down I tuck my left leg under the chair like that, and stretch my right leg out in front.

ROSA: Yes. I wasn't thinking. What it means is that you'll have to tuck your right leg under, and stick the left leg forward.

[PASQUALE *enters in his pyjamas. He is rather the worse for wear, and looks older than his fifty years.*]

PASQUALE: Is there a drink of water?

MARIA: You've got water! I put a whole glass full by your bed last night! You can't have drunk it all!

MATHILDE: I suppose you heard the alarm go off.

PASQUALE: Is that what it was?

MATHILDE: You know perfectly well it was.

PASQUALE: I'm a light sleeper! The slightest noise and I'm wide awake. You know that. If you don't, it's time you did. You ought to know by now what state my nerves are in.

MATHILDE: And having conveniently woken up, you come prying in here.

PASQUALE: Prying? What is there to come prying about?

MATHILDE: To see what I'm having done to my dress! That's what.

PASQUALE: I see. And that's none of my business, I suppose. It's none of my business what you and this scatter-brained trollop of a sister of

mine are cooking up between you to entertain
your clients with! It's all right for those half-
witted louts to gawp at you in it and get a
cheap thrill, but I'm not allowed to have any
say in the matter.

MATHILDE: How do you want me to receive clients, then?
Dressed like a nun?

ROSA: She needs something a little bit striking.

MARIA: Men talk among themselves. Word soon gets
round.

PASQUALE: [*goes into his patter*] 'Step this way, gentlemen.
Come and get an eyeful of Pasquale Cim-
maruta's wife this morning. She's showing
her legs today, and if your eyesight's good
enough, you'll be able to see her bare breasts.'

MATHILDE: Bare breasts? What bare breasts? This, I'll
have you know, is pink silk!

PASQUALE: *It's flesh-coloured*!

ROSA: What if it is flesh-coloured?

PASQUALE: You can hold your tongue!

MATHILDE: All right, then. I'll ask you. What if it is flesh-
coloured?

PASQUALE: In the half-light? With you sitting at the back
of the room? In your gilt chair? And every
client who comes in sitting there goggle-eyed
…squirming about in his chair…trying to
make out whether it's bare flesh or only pink
silk?

MATHILDE: If that's the way his mind's working, it's his
affair. That's all I can say. Someone's got to
bring some money into the house. If you don't
like the way I do it, why don't you go out and
earn some yourself? Then you might have
some room to talk! What a man! My God…!
[*She goes out.*]

PASQUALE: And aren't I bringing money in? It's not a bed
of roses for me, either. I'm aching so much at

the end of the day, it's all I can do sometimes to crawl into bed.

ROSA: Why don't you go back and lie down, and have your sleep out. You can eat your breakfast later.

PASQUALE: Yes. I'll go back to bed. I don't mind suffering the torments of the damned. I'm used enough to it by now.

[*He goes out.*]

ROSA: Poor Pasquale…

MARIA: He'll end up in the madhouse if he's not careful.

[*The doorbell sounds.*]

Whoever could that be at this time?

ROSA: Well, don't just stand there! Go and see.

[MARIA *goes out and comes back.*]

MARIA: It's don Carlo from across the landing.

ROSA: Don Carlo? What does don Carlo want at this hour in the morning?

MARIA: I think he's been taken ill. He just collapsed straight into a chair, and he's sitting mopping his face out there with a handkerchief.

[ROSA *crosses to the door and speaks through it.*]

ROSA: Don Carlo…whatever's the matter? Come in. Maria will help you. [*to* MARIA] Give don Carlo a hand, Maria.

[MARIA *goes out and comes back in supporting* CARLO, *who is walking with difficulty.*]

MARIA: Just take it slowly…that's right…hold on to my arm…[*to* ROSA]…I think he's just come over dizzy.

CARLO: One minute I was as right as rain, coming up the stairs, and then suddenly, without any warning…

ROSA: Come over here and sit down.

[*He sits, helped by* MARIA.]
Perhaps you'd like Maria to get you a glass of water.

CARLO: No! Not water. Water would do more harm than good. I'm perspiring. It feels as if I'd got a blindfold on. I was reaching up to ring our doorbell...you know the brass lion's head we've got with the bell-push in its nose...but before I could get my finger to it, everything suddenly went black and the stairs started going round and round, and it felt as if I was being plunged down into some sort of abyss. If I hadn't managed to clutch hold of the stair rail, I'd have gone hurtling down to the bottom and ended up with my head in the dustbin.

MARIA: It sounds to me as if you'd eaten something.

CARLO: Yes. I was wondering about that.

ROSA: What did you have to eat yesterday?

CARLO: Well, normally I eat very little. I'm a frugal eater in the normal way. But my brother... Alberto...goes mad every so often and comes in laden. We're on our own, as you know, so it's just the two of us...Alberto and me... there are no women in the house...so we don't bother all that much as a rule about cooking. It's different when there's a whole family to cook for...you'd know all about that being housewives...but for just the two of you it's a nuisance, and no cheaper than getting it ready-cooked from Marco's. So that's what we usually do. But, as I say, yesterday Alberto went a bit mad and came back laden with stuff and I think we may have overdone it a bit. We had a quarter of a pound of olives, and a whole pig's trotter, just between the two of us, and I'm ashamed to say we wolfed the lot. You know how it is...he'd have an olive, and

I'd have an olive...and then we'd start in on the pig's trotter...chatting away about this and that, as you do...and before we knew where we were, there was nothing but a few scraps left behind. When you're having a pleasant evening and enjoying one another's company, you don't notice how much you're putting away.

MARIA: And that was the entire meal? For the two of you? A quarter of a pound of olives and a pig's trotter!

CARLO: Yes. It's too much for an evening meal. It's why I came over faint this morning. I went out at seven as I always do for early mass...I never miss early mass...and it was when I got back that I felt it. The reason I rang your doorbell was so as not to alarm Alberto. I was sure you wouldn't mind.

ROSA: Of course not. It's a pleasure to be able to help.

CARLO: What I would be grateful for is a glass of wine. I think it might be just what I need to put me on my feet.

ROSA: Yes. Bring the wine over, Maria.

[MARIA *does so and pours some wine into a glass for* CARLO.]

MARIA: There. Drink that.

CARLO: Thank you.

[ROSA *notices the macaroni and rushes over to it.*]

ROSA: Oh, no! Now look what's happened! He won't eat that now.

CARLO: What is it? What's happened?

ROSA: It's just some macaroni I was heating up from yesterday. It's for my nephew. He likes macaroni, and now I've burnt it. For the second time.

CARLO: You're not going to throw it away?

ROSA: That's what comes of not keeping my mind on what I was doing.

> [*She takes the earthenware dish off the gas ring.*]

CARLO: Can I look? [*He looks.*] Oh, yes…It'd be a shame to waste that. [*He takes a fork.*] Is this clean?

ROSA: What? Yes.

CARLO: Do you mind if I try some?

ROSA: Go ahead.

> [CARLO *tastes a forkful.*]

CARLO: It's not at all bad. It's a bit burnt in places, but it's not bad. I tell you what…if your nephew doesn't want to eat it…I'd be quite happy to finish it up for you, because I'm beginning to wonder whether this glass of wine on an empty stomach is a good idea. It might just bring on the dizziness again.

ROSA: Help yourself. Finish the lot.

> [CARLO *takes the dish to the table, and gets down to it greedily.* ROSA *and* MARIA *exchange glances.*]

I shall have to get a couple of eggs and scramble those for Luigi instead.

CARLO: *Two* eggs! My word! You do yourselves well!

> [*He goes on eating.*]

ROSA: They're not that hard to come by!

CARLO: True…and with what don Pasquale brings in, I expect you can afford it.

ROSA: Don Pasquale…? Yes, he manages, I suppose.

CARLO: [*still eating*] Your sister-in-law can't be doing badly, either. She's no sooner finished with one client than there's another one waiting on the doorstep. I'm often saying to Alberto what a luxury it must be to be able to afford to have two eggs every day for breakfast.

ROSA: But what about the displays...surely there's money coming in from that?

CARLO: There was. When our father was alive. Saporito was a name to be reckoned with in those days. In those days you couldn't put on a show with a performing monkey in a side street without you hired a set of chairs from Tommaso Saporito. Illuminations for Easter Week...it was always Tommaso Saporito you came to as a matter of coure. Somebody wanting to open a bathing beach out at Santa Lucia, the first thing he'd do would be to come and see Tommaso Saporito about the hire of tables. But that's all changed now. The big combines have taken over. The days are gone now when two or three of you could get together and arrange everything over a glass of wine. It takes a full-scale cabinet meeting with three Prime Ministers and half a dozen heads of state presiding over it nowadays every time you want to organise a street party in an alleyway somewhere. Everywhere you go, it's the big fish eating up the little fish. The only way Alberto and I have managed to keep our heads above water is by getting rid of the stock...selling it off bit by bit. All that's left is a few bits of carpet. That and a hundred or so chairs. It's enough to make you weep, seeing it all go. I suppose we should be thankful we've still got our eyes left to weep with. It's still possible to make money, donna Rosa, if you're not too overburdened with scruples, but if you're honest these days, you starve.

ROSA: And what's that meant to imply? That because we occasionally have two eggs for breakfast we're hardened criminals?

CARLO: [*mock-jokingly*] Well...if the cap fits...

ROSA: The cap doesn't fit!

CARLO: Don't take it to heart, donna Rosa. I was only joking. [*He eyes the plums.*] These look tempting.

ROSA: Yes.

CARLO: You wouldn't begrudge me a bite from one of these, would you.

> [ROSA *snatches up the dish of plums and thrusts it in front of* CARLO.]

ROSA: Here! Help yourself!

> [CARLO *carefully selects the best.*]

CARLO: This one looks as if it'll be past its best if it's not eaten soon. [*He bites into it.*] Tell me something. Why have you decided to move out?

ROSA: Decided to do what?

CARLO: Someone was mentioning last night that you'd packed your things and were moving out.

ROSA: Well, I don't know who it was, but they told you wrong.

CARLO: I can't remember now who it was.

> [CARLO *is on his third plum, and* ROSA *snatches the plate away from him and puts it back where it was.*]

ROSA: Do you mind...! My brother's been waiting for those!

CARLO: Just as well to put them out of reach. I'd probably have finished the lot.

ROSA: So I could see.

MARIA: You've been starving yourself. That's why you were taken ill on the stairs. It's not eating properly that brings it on.

> [*The doorbell sounds.*]

ROSA: See who that is.

> [MARIA *goes out and comes back in with* ALBERTO. *He is a man bowed down beneath the burden of fifty years of a hard life. He is pale and gaunt. He has on a worn and faded suit and carries a gnarled*

*walking stick over his left arm. He is
agitated and keeps glancing nervously at
his watch all through what follows.*]

ALBERTO: Carlo! The last place I expected to find you!
[*He rushes to* CARLO.] What happened?

CARLO: It's nothing to get alarmed about, Albe. I'm
all right again now.

ALBERTO: Donna Rosa…good morning. [*to* CARLO] But
what happened?

CARLO: Well…one minute I was fine, and then…

ALBERTO: How are you now?

CARLO: I've told you, Albe. I'm perfectly all right.

ALBERTO: I was worried about you. When you hadn't
come home, I looked out of the window, but
there was no sign of you, so I asked Michele if
he'd seen anything of you, and he said he saw
you come in over a quarter of an hour ago, so I
rang the bell here in case they knew where
you were. The last thing I expected was to
find you actually in here. What was it? A
dizzy spell?

CARLO: I suddenly came over faint. My legs just
seemed to give way underneath me.

ALBERTO: Yes, I know. I'm not feeling any too well
myself. I had a bad night. Have they given
you any coffee?

MARIA: I'll tell you what he's had, if you want to know
what he's had. He's had a whole saucepan full
of burnt macaroni, one glass of wine, and
three plums!

[MARIA *goes out left as* ROSA *goes out by
the other door.*]

CARLO: And that's me finished for the day. Nothing
more now till tomorrow. [*to* ALBERTO] Have
you done it?

[ALBERTO *makes sure they are alone.*]

ALBERTO: Yes. I've given them a signed statement, and
they're coming round here in ten minutes. In

the meantime, we're to see that no one goes out.

[ROSA *returns*.]

Is don Pasquale awake?

ROSA: Not as far as I know.

ALBERTO: He's lucky to be able to sleep. What about your sister-in-law, donna Mathilde? Is she asleep too? And your nephew and his sister?

ROSA: At half past seven in the morning, it's not all that uncommon for people to be sleeping!

ALBERTO: Yes...but if you're moving out...

ROSA: Moving out? What is all this about moving out?

ALBERTO: It's what someone was saying. So...the Cimmaruta family are all sleeping soundly in their beds as if they hadn't a care in the world.

ROSA: They're sleeping like anybody else. Why? Is there some reason why they shouldn't be?

[MARIA *comes back in*.]

ALBERTO: No, no. By no means. I suppose I can't help feeling a touch of envy. I can't remember when I last had a good night's sleep.

ROSA: You sound as if you've got something on your conscience that's troubling you.

ALBERTO: No. There's nothing on my conscience. My conscience is perfectly clear. My conscience is as spotless and unblemished as the handkerchief in the Immaculate Virgin's right hand.

CARLO: Or left hand.

ROSA: In that case, if you're not sleeping, it's because there's something else wrong with you.

MARIA: You want to take a laxative.

ALBERTO: No. It's not anything to do with that. Carlo knows why I can't sleep. Too many things passing through my mind. You lie there turning things over and over. When our father died...Carlo knows this...he died happy because he thought he was leaving us well provided for, with a thriving business that would see us out and our children as well. Instead of that, here we are. Living from hand to mouth. Never sure from one day to another where the next meal's coming from. I know what you're going to say. Why don't you take up some other line of business. But what is there I could do...with a constitution that's not worth twopence...? How can you apply yourself to anything? Business calls for a cool head and calm nerves. There are times, donna Rosa, when for two pins I'd throw it all in and present myself to my Maker without waiting to be summoned.

CARLO: Alberto! Please. You know I don't like to hear you blaspheming like that. We shall just have to part company if you will keep doing it.

[PASQUALE *comes in, sleepy and irritated. He is in his shirtsleeves and carrying his jacket, tie and hat.*]

PASQUALE: Rosa...see if you can get this stain out for me, will you? [*He shows her a stain on the lapel of his jacket, then sees* CARLO *and* ALBERTO.] Oh...good morning.

ALBERTO: Good morning.

PASQUALE: My daughter gave me one of those liqueur chocolates with liquid in it without telling me what it was, and I bit into it and it's spurted out on to the lapel of my jacket. Some of it went on my tie as well. [*He hands the tie to* MARIA.] See what you can do with it, Maria. [*to* ALBERTO *and* CARLO] And to what are we indebted for a visit so early in the morning?

ALBERTO: Nothing to be alarmed about.

ROSA: Don Carlo was taken ill on the stairs.

PASQUALE: Yes. I've seen this coming. You should look

after yourself more. If you don't take care
you'll find yourself in the next world before
your time.

CARLO: I hope it won't come to that.

PASQUALE: Yes...hope...that's it. Hope is the one thing
that keeps us going. We can't do without
hope.

> [*He drinks the coffee* ROSA *has brought
> him.*]

ROSA: What's wrong? Couldn't you get back to sleep
again?

PASQUALE: I'm on my way out. I'm meeting someone at
the station.

> [ALBERTO *and* CARLO *exchange
> glances.*]

ALBERTO: So you *are* moving out, then?

PASQUALE: Moving out?

ALBERTO: It was going round the building last night
that you were moving out, and then when I
asked donna Rosa, she denied all knowledge
of it, and now you say you're off to the station,
so I take it the rumours are correct.

PASQUALE: No. They're not correct.

ALBERTO: But I thought I understood you to say you
were setting off by train somewhere...

PASQUALE: I happen to have an appointment to meet
someone at the station! It's a convenient
place to meet! It doesn't mean I'm moving
my entire family out. Trains have got nothing
to do with it!

ALBERTO: Ah...I get it now. You're meeting someone
outside the station in Garibaldi Square. I
understand now. But it's freezing out. You
know how the wind whistles across the square
there when it's at all blustery. Why not put it
off? It's not as if it's vital.

PASQUALE: Look...do I have to come and consult you

before I'm allowed to step outside my own house?

ALBERTO: No, no. That's not what I meant at all. But what's wrong with having a quiet morning at home? There's nothing I like better personally than pottering around...having a go at all the various odd jobs that accumulate. They're a nuisance, but once they're done, they're done...things like moving that picture on to the other wall, for instance...or shifting this carpet a bit further that way...rearranging the furniture and putting some of it in the other room...moving the cupboard across to the other wall...that sort of thing...

PASQUALE: I see. So I'm to get out of bed and start shifting furniture around.

ALBERTO: Not all of it. Just the odd thing here and there. That dresser, for instance. You'd get a far better effect with it if it were standing in the space there behind the door. In fact...Carlo... come and give me a hand and we'll move it across for him.

[*He crosses to the dresser to move it.*]

PASQUALE: Oh, no! The dresser stays where it is, thank you very much. It's been put there for a reason.

ALBERTO: Aha! Did you hear that, Carlo? They have a reason for wanting it there.

CARLO: And we can guess what the reason is.

PASQUALE: The reason is that I like it there! It's my dresser, and it's in my house! Do I come into your house and start moving furniture about?

ALBERTO: If you want to come over and shift furniture, you're welcome to at any time. People are free to rearrange furniture whenever the spirit moves them. I don't stand on ceremony about things like that. It's open house. Come and

move some now. There's no time like the
present.

PASQUALE: Don Alberto, I don't know what all this is
about, but I've had a dreadful night...

ALBERTO: That's exactly what I was saying just now to
donna Rosa. Sleep has become a luxury these
days. Far too much going on up here...[*He
touches his forehead.*]...don Pasquale, isn't
there? You no sooner put your head on the
pillow than it's in a turmoil. All the things
you've been keeping bottled up inside you
during the day start to come out at night and
prey on your mind so that you can't sleep.

PASQUALE: There's nothing whatever preying on my
mind, don Alberto. The only reason I can't
sleep is that...I can't sleep. I've never gone
into the reason.

ALBERTO: Could it be because there are so many people
who are not amongst us any more? People
who are no longer in the land of the living.
Just think how many millions of them there
are. They far outnumber the rest of us who
are still here.

PASQUALE: Considering people have been dying since
time immemorial, it's hardly surprising!

ALBERTO: True. But there are dead people and dead
people, don Pasquale.

PASQUALE: There are people whose lives have come to an
end. Those are the only dead people I know
anything about.

ALBERTO: Ah...but you're talking about people who've
died a natural death, and can rest in peace.
Who don't come back to haunt us. But what
about the ones who die before their time, don
Pasquale? The ones who've been helped on
their way? The ones whose spirits remain...
hovering...who are all around us...in the
chairs...in the furniture. At night, you hear a

creak…a groan…a door slowly opens as if a ghostly hand had done it…you feel strange, eerie sensations at night under your pillow… in your clothes…the feeling of things lurking there…nudging you…unable to find rest…and then, when everything's silent, an unearthly shriek rends the air. Those are the dead people I'm talking about, don Pasquale. They're the reason there's no sleeping peacefully at night.

> [*The doorbell sounds. It brings them all back to earth with a start and a sense of relief.* PASQUALE *goes back out the way he came in.*]

ROSA: See who that is, Maria.

> [MARIA *goes out, followed by* ALBERTO.]

We were in a reasonably cheerful mood before don Alberto came in.

ALBERTO: [*off*] They're here, Carlo!

> [CARLO *suddenly jumps up and grabs* ROSA, *holding her firmly by the arms.*]

CARLO: Don't make a sound! Commend your soul to Almighty God, and pray that He will be merciful. [*Shouting*] Come in, Albe!

ROSA: For the love of God, what on earth is going on?

> [ALBERTO *comes in with* MARIA *in a firm grip. He is followed by* MICHELE *and a local Chief of Security of the rank of* LIEUTENANT, *who is in uniform and accompanied by five* CARABINIERI, *all armed with pistols and machine-guns. Three of them block the exits.*]

LIEUTENANT: [*to a* CARABINIERE] You. Don't move from there. [*to the others*] You, come with me.

> [*They go out left into the other part of the house.*]

ALBERTO: At last! The moment of retribution has

arrived! An innocent man's blood is about to
be avenged!

> [ROSA *and* MARIA *protest in outrage and
> astonishment.*]

CARLO: Commend yourselves to Almighty God, and
pray that He will be merciful.

> [*Offstage an infernal din has broken out.
> Shouts, screams, protests. Then the*
> CARABINIERI *come in dragging* PAS-
> QUALE, MATHILDE, ELVIRA *and* LUIGI.
> *The latter are asleep and half-dressed.*
> PASQUALE *is beside himself with rage.*]

PASQUALE: Has everyone gone stark raving mad? [*to*
LIEUTENANT] Who are you?

LIEUTENANT: You'll find out soon enough.

MATHILDE: Dragging us out of bed as if we were criminals...! I'm not even decent!

ALBERTO: Decent? What's decency to someone like you?
You don't know the meaning of the word
decency!

> [LUIGI *hurls himself on* ALBERTO, *and
> has to be restrained by a* CARABINIERE.]

LUIGI: You shut your filthy mouth, you doddering
old cretin!

ALBERTO: And as for you, you're nothing but a common
murderer. Like your father there, and your
mother. And your sister and your aunt. And
this depraved specimen as well that you have
about the place to keep house for you.

> [*The* CIMMARUTAS *stand there speechless
> with dumbfounded outrage.*]

Here you have them, Lieutenant. Unmasked
for what they are. A pack of murdering swine.
Don't be taken in by their innocent looks. It's
all down there in the signed statement...*and* I
know where to put my hand on the evidence.
There's no wriggling out of it, although
they'd like to. [*indicating* PASQUALE] This

monster of depravity...who'd like you to think of him as a devoted father, with no thought in his head except to give his two children a good education and look after his family, spends his time watching his wife indulge in one sordid affair after another with a stream of callers who queue up for her favours under pretence of having their fortunes told!

[LUIGI *struggles to get at* ALBERTO.]

LUIGI: We don't have to listen to this filthy-minded old sod...!

ALBERTO: There's no point in getting worked up. It won't make the slightest difference. There's plenty of proof. I've been keeping watch, and following your movements, and my suspicions have all been confirmed. These loathsome reptiles, lieutenant, are the perpetrators of a crime that it'd make your blood run cold to think about. With this hussy here...[*indicating* MATHILDE]...as bait, they enticed my friend Aniello Amitrano into the house and then, once he was inside, they slit his throat, robbed him of everything he possessed, and then disposed of the body.

[*They all protest in bewildered anger.*]

But God is not mocked. Murder does not go unpunished. They thought they'd hidden the evidence away where no one could find it till it was too late and they'd made their getaway, but I know where it is and when the miserable reptiles are confronted with it, they'll have no choice but to come clean. Take them away, lieutenant.

LIEUTENANT: Right. Come on. All of you.

PASQUALE: The man's a raving lunatic! We're perfectly respectable people...!

LIEUTENANT: Come on. Outside. Quickly.

[*The* CARABINIERI *push the family out, all protesting, and are followed by* CARLO, *who is murmuring about trusting themselves to God.*]

[*to* ALBERTO] We'll expect you down there with the evidence in fifteen minutes.

[*He goes out, pushing* PASQUALE.]

ALBERTO: Yes. Off you go. One clean sweep with the lot of them.

MICHELE: Who'd ever have dreamt there was anything like that going on? Where did they hide it, then, the evidence…?

ALBERTO: Behind the dresser there. In a cavity in the wall. They took out some bricks, stuffed the evidence in the hole, and then moved the dresser in front of it until they could plaster it over. That was going to be their last job this morning before they left if we hadn't forestalled them. There's the shirt in there all covered with blood that he had on when they clubbed him to death…

MICHELE: I thought you said they slit his throat.

ALBERTO: …that's right…and one of his shoes and some papers. Come and give me a hand to move this out of the way, and we'll see what else they've hidden there as well.

[*They move the dresser, but there is nothing but bare wall, untampered with.*]

Oh. Well, then, if it's not there, it must be over here.

[*He crosses to another part of the kitchen and rips a shelf off the wall, bringing saucepans and frying pans down with it. He looks everywhere, but there is nothing.*]

Not there either. In that case, there's only one place it can be. Under the coal. Where do they keep their coal?

MICHELE: They don't have coal. They do all their cooking by gas.

ALBERTO: Are you sure?

MICHELE: Of course I'm sure.

ALBERTO: I don't know where it can be, then. Unless it's in that basket.

MICHELE: You only think it might be there?

> [ALBERTO *looks, without much conviction, and again draws a blank.*]

ALBERTO: Do you know what, Michele?

MICHELE: No, don Alberto, I don't.

ALBERTO: I'm not sure I didn't dream the whole thing.

MICHELE: *Dream* it?

ALBERTO: It was so vivid.

MICHELE: *Now* you think you dreamt it...?

ALBERTO: Be a good chap and get me a glass of water, Michele, would you?

MICHELE: [*going*] *Now* he says he dreamt it!

> [ALBERTO *stands there musing.*]

ALBERTO: What a dream! What an extraordinary dream!

> [*A look of something like ecstasy gradually comes over his face.*]

What an absolutely magnificent dream!

ACT TWO

Interior of the Saporitos' apartment: an enormous room with a door, left, leading into the rest of the apartment, and a door, right, leading into the hall. The room is full of old junk of all kinds. Chairs are piled up on top of one another in every corner of the room, and hang in bunches from the ceiling. There are lengths of rolled-up carpet tied round with string. The place is festooned with oil-lamp illuminations such as were used for fêtes in the alleyways of Naples. Banners, plumes, carnival lights, paper flowers, saints, holy pictures, fireworks of all shapes and sizes and colours are nailed to a piece of wood in one part of the room. There is a rough, hand-made ladder leading up to a gallery on which a rickety old gilded sofa serves ZI NICOLA *as a bed. His privacy is preserved by a screen made up of old rags and bits of curtain and a large enamel plate advertising some pharmaceutical product. Everything is overlaid by a thick coating of dirt and dust. A large window high up lets in some light through its dirty panes.*

It is afternoon. ZI NICOLA *is up in his gallery, busy with his own affairs, and sticking his head out every so often from behind the curtain to spit.* CARLO *is at a table making an inventory on a page torn from an old exercise book of everything in the room, while* CAPA D'ANGELO, *a dealer in secondhand furniture, assesses the value of everything.*

CARLO: Including the ones in the other room, that's four hundred and fifty chairs altogether.
  [ZI NICOLA *spits.*]
  Watch where you're spitting, Nicola. Remember we're underneath!

CAPA: It was a miracle that missed me!

CARLO: He's getting on. You have to humour him.

CAPA: You've told him three times since I've been
here not to spit. Doesn't he understand a
word you say to him?

CARLO: Oh, yes. He understands.

CAPA: Why does he never answer?

CARLO: He can't.

CAPA: Is he dumb?

CARLO: No, it's not that. It's a bit of a long story. It's
not so much that he can't talk, as that he
won't. He gave it up when he decided it was a
waste of time. Humanity's deaf, so why
bother talking to it. That's the way he sees it.
Besides which, he doesn't think he's got the
vocabulary. So he lets off fireworks instead,
and expresses himself that way. Give him a
thunderflash and two or three catherine
wheels, and he can be surprisingly eloquent.
It's why they call him the gunpowder poet.
Every bang a sonnet.

CAPA: Unusual, isn't it?

CARLO: He's an unusual character.

CAPA: How does anyone manage to understand
him?

CARLO: No one does, except my brother. Alberto can
understand every word he says. I can make
out one or two things. 'Give me a glass of
water' I know...that's two bangs and a
whizz-whizz. Three bangs and then another
bang with a sort of whistle in the middle
means 'What's the time?' If he wants to let
you know he's ready for something to eat, it's
one bang with a whistle in the middle and
then a whizz-whizz and three more bangs.

CAPA: And your brother manages to understand all
that.

CARLO: Oh, yes. They carry on long conversations.
They're chewing the fat for hours on end

CAPA: sometimes. It's like a carnival in here when they really get going...smoke everywhere.

CAPA: It sounds pretty crazy to me.

CARLO: Someone came in not long ago wanting some fireworks for his wife's birthday...ready to spend the earth if necessary...but he had to go off empty-handed. Zi Nicola couldn't spare the time. He's busy up there making a special Roman candle to let off when he dies. It's green. It has to be green.

CAPA: Why does it?

CARLO: Green for go.

CAPA: Oh.

CARLO: According to him, dying's the one thing you don't have to have a licence for.

CAPA: Yes.

CARLO: I told you he had some odd ideas.

CAPA: So he's the gunpowder poet...

CARLO: Anyway...four hundred and fifty chairs...

CAPA: If you can call them chairs. There isn't a sound one amongst them.

CARLO: Oh. I'm sorry. I've made a mistake. I thought I was talking to someone who knew what he was about. I thought I was talking to someone who could recognise quality when he saw it. Look at that. Look at the way that's finished off. That was made at the Nunziata in the days of old-fashioned craftsmanship when a chair was a chair. You won't find that turning to matchwood the minute you sit on it. That's a relic of the days when people took a pride in their work.

CAPA: Relic is the word.

CARLO: My father...Tommaso Saporito...would take his hat off to these chairs. If he happened to have a hat on. If not, he'd take off what he did have on. If he was wearing a beret, he'd take that off. They'd only have to be so much as mentioned, and off it'd come.

CAPA: So what am I supposed to do?

CARLO: We're talking about chairs here that are worth every bit of fifty lire apiece!

CAPA: Don Carlo. You're talking to Cicillo Capa d'Angelo...from the Piazza Francese... Nannina Zupperelle's son...don't try and teach me my business. These...fifty lire apiece...? They're not worth fifty lire the lot! It's junk!

CARLO: These chairs...

CAPA: Look...I'll tell you what we'll do. To save time and do you a favour, I'll take the chairs and anything else you want to throw in as a job lot.

CARLO: Oh, no! Oh, no! We value it item by item, or there's nothing doing.

CAPA: Listen. I'm a busy man. Do you want to sell, or don't you?

CARLO: That depends. On a certain eventuality.

CAPA: Right. Well, when a certain eventuality turns up, whatever it is, come and see me and we'll bring a handcart round and load the whole lot on to it and I'll give you fifty thousand lire... into your hand in thousand lire notes...on the spot there and then...and we'll call it a deal.

CARLO: You're joking! Fifty thousand lire? The carpets alone are worth more than that!

CAPA: These moth-eaten bits of old sacking? They're falling to pieces. It's only the dust on them that's holding them together. That and the spittle.

CARLO: The spittle's beside the point. I'm not talking about the spittle, I'm talking about the carpets, and you're not coming here...

CAPA: Look...I've got some stuff to see over at

Salvator Rosa's. If you've made up your mind
when I get back...

CARLO: Nothing's going out of here for less than two
hundred and fifty thousand lire.

CAPA: Seventy. That's my last offer. Seventy-five
thousand lire...take it or leave it. It's a load of
old junk.

[CAPA D'ANGELO *goes out, followed by*
CARLO.]

CARLO: You don't have to take it! Nobody's holding a
pistol to your head! You expect to get Paris...
with Rome and Florence thrown in...for the
price of a box of matches!

CAPA: It's not Paris I'm buying!

[ZI NICOLA *comes down the ladder. He
crosses wearily to a corner of the room,
rummages in a pile of rubbish and pulls out
a length of cord knotted in several loops.
Then he looks around for a glass, finds one,
fills it to the brim with some cloudy wine
from a lopsided flask, and goes back up the
ladder. When he gets to the top he goes
behind the curtain, then, lifting one corner
of it, looks out and spits down, and disap-
pears again.* CARLO *comes back in, crosses
to the table, and begins carefully arranging
papers on it.*]

ALBERTO: [*off*] Carlo...!

CARLO: Albe...!

[ALBERTO   *comes   in,   followed   by*
MICHELE.]

What have you let us in for, Albe?

ALBERTO: I had no alternative, Carlo. I did what I saw
as my duty.

CARLO: So what do we do now?

ALBERTO: There's nothing we can do. We shall just have
to wait and see what happens.

[*He sits down dejectedly.*]

MICHELE: I was absolutely thunderstruck when I saw them all come trooping back. It was like a funeral procession. The whole family. Don Pasquale looking like death...not saying a word...his wife as well...'I won't be receiving clients today, Michele'...and then the rest of them following one another up the stairs. They went inside and shut the door, and there hasn't been a sound from them since.

CARLO: You managed to speak to the Commissioner of Police...

ALBERTO: Yes. I made a formal declaration...not a shred of evidence...no papers...no proof... I'd been to them and reported a crime that had never taken place...and wasn't at all sure I hadn't dreamt it.

CARLO: Do you mean you're not even sure now whether it was a dream?

ALBERTO: I'm pretty sure. I couldn't be absolutely certain. I'm hazy about it, Carlo. The Commissioner was as taken aback as you are. I got a very old-fashioned look from him. He said 'I thought I'd heard everything.' I believe he was wondering if I was all there. Then he made me go and wait outside, and eventually the lieutenant came out and said I could go for the time being, and said he hoped for my sake the water I was in would be fairly lukewarm.

CARLO: What did he mean by lukewarm?

ALBERTO: Not too hot.

CARLO: You'll be in trouble, though.

ALBERTO: That goes without saying.

MICHELE: It's nothing to what you're going to be in for when the Cimmarutas hear you're back.

ALBERTO: What do you mean?

MICHELE: I mean that if I were in their shoes I'd wait till I'd got you outside and then I'd kick your

	teeth in. After that, I'd feel better.
ALBERTO:	Yes. That had occurred to me.
CARLO:	And me.
ALBERTO:	We all seem of the same mind on that score. Michele…I wonder if you'd do something for me. Go down to Vicolo Lammatari…number fifteen on the third floor…and ask if Aniello Amitrano came home last night.
MICHELE:	Well, I'll have to do it now if I'm going to do it…I shan't have time later. But if you take my advice, you'll stay indoors, don Alberto, out of don Pasquale's way, or he'll give you a going-over that'll alter your landscape a bit.

[MICHELE *goes out.*]

CARLO:	Albe…my dear old brother…why don't we sit down and have a little chat…?
ALBERTO:	What about?
MICHELE:	[*off*] Oh…come in, lieutenant.

[MICHELE *comes back in, followed by the*
LIEUTENANT.]

The lieutenant to see you.

CARLO:	This is it. He's come to take you in.
LIEUTENANT:	Don Alberto. I wonder if I could sit down for a moment. It's been an exhausting day.
ALBERTO:	Of course. Have a chair.
LIEUTENANT:	[*sits*] Well…there's no point in beating about the bush…
CARLO:	What did I tell you?
LIEUTENANT:	It's out of the hands now of the Commissioner and it's being dealt with by the Public Prosecutor.
CARLO:	They're taking a serious view of it, then.
LIEUTENANT:	He's asked for your affidavit, and he's looking at it now. If he takes the view that you were acting in good faith, it's more than likely he'll let the matter drop. But, if he comes to the conclusion that there's something a bit fishy going on, as he probably will, there'll be a

warrant issued for your arrest and I shall
have no alternative but to come round and
take you back to police headquarters.

ALBERTO: Something fishy. I see. We've reached the
point now when we're not allowed to dream
any longer.

LIEUTENANT: You're perfectly at liberty to dream, don
Alberto, but we've got the job of deciding
whether it really was a dream, or whether
there's more to it. We can't rule out the possibility that you've been got at to change your
story, for instance. It's not unknown.

ALBERTO: I can set your mind at rest on that score here
and now.

LIEUTENANT: That's all right. We'll set our own minds at
rest, don Alberto. What I came here for was
to warn you not to go out in case I have to
come back for you. I need to know where I
can find you. And, if I were you, I'd keep well
out of don Pasquale's way as well. They
might well decide to take the law into their
own hands, and I can't say I'd altogether
blame them.

CARLO: What's the position there? Can they, if they
beat him up, take legal action as well?

ALBERTO: One or the other! They can't beat me up *and*
take legal action!

LIEUTENANT: I wouldn't bank on it too much. I can tell you
one thing for sure. If it does end up in court, I
wouldn't be any too sanguine about your
chances of getting off lightly. They'd go for
very heavy damages, and probably get them.

CARLO: Would it mean a prison sentence for him?

LIEUTENANT: That's up to the court. All I can do is give you
a friendly warning as to what you might be in
for, if they do issue a warrant, that's all. And
to tell you to stay put so I shall know where to
find you.

ALBERTO: Yes. I shall be here.

LIEUTENANT: I'll say good evening, then.

[*He goes.* MICHELE *follows.*]

MICHELE: I'll go to...Vicolo Lammatari...

CARLO: Well. You've really let us in for it this time.

ALBERTO: You always look on the black side, Carlo. It's not as bad as all that. I acted with the best of intentions. It's not as if I've killed anybody.

CARLO: Albe...It's in the hands of the Public Prosecutor! It's a serious offence to bring an accusation against somebody without evidence to back it up. You've got to face the truth, Albe. You're going to end up in the dock. You could get five years.

ALBERTO: If it were that serious, why would they have let me come home?

CARLO: In order to put you off the scent. While they're making investigations. It's obvious. You heard what the lieutenant said. You're virtually under house arrest, Albe. That's what it amounts to. I don't think you begin to realise what a serious matter it is...especially for me.

ALBERTO: You? How do you come into it?

CARLO: It's always worse for the other person, Albe, you know that.

ALBERTO: What other person? You're not implicated.

CARLO: Certainly not. I had no hand in it whatsoever. But you've got to consider my position. You don't imagine I'm looking forward to being pointed at in the street? As the brother of a gaolbird. I take my position in society seriously, Albe. It's the stigma. And not only the stigma. You realise, don't you, that you'll never be able to hold public office? That you'll be treated as an outcast? And me with you. It all rubs off, Albe. We're both of us finished so far as holding our heads up in public is concerned.

ALBERTO: Carlo…what's all this leading up to?

CARLO: It's not leading up to anything, Albe. I just want us to come to some arrangement so that if the worst should come to the worst, we're in a position to take care of ourselves. It's simply making provision.

ALBERTO: I thought it was something like that.

CARLO: Why don't we sit down quietly, Albe, and I'll tell you what I've got worked out. There's quite a nice bit of capital tied up here.…[*He gestures round the room.*]…which belongs to both of us…and what I've done is to draw up this document…which only needs your signature…giving me the right in your 'absence'…I haven't specified what the absence is…to make whatever use of it I think best, without having to come to you about it every time. Because what's going to happen, Albe, is that someone'll come in wanting a couple of hundred chairs in a hurry, for a fête somewhere, and with you in gaol my hands are going to be tied.

ALBERTO: You're determined to look on the black side, Carlo. It hasn't come to that yet. It probably never will. In fact, strangely enough, I've rarely felt in a more tranquil frame of mind.

CARLO: All right. We'll sit back and do nothing. We'll pretend it's all a figment of my imagination, and carry on as if nothing had happened.

ALBERTO: I'm not saying it's a figment of your imagination, Carlo. But it's not necessary to rush into things. We've got plenty of time before we have to come to any decisions about things like that. If anything like that has to be done, we'll do it when they come to arrest me. That'll be soon enough.

CARLO: And then you'll give me carte blanche…

ALBERTO: A completely free hand. To do as you like. But
wait till it's happened. Then you can start
making 'arrangements'.

CARLO: If that's how you want it.

ALBERTO: What a farcical situation it is, when you come
to think about it! I have a dream and then I
can't be sure whether it was a dream, or
whether it actually happened. The strange
thing is, it's all so vivid. There's such a wealth
of detail. I can see it now as clearly as I can see
you. I can see where they hid the shirt, I can
see the bloodstains on it, I can see the shoe,
and yet when we came to look there was nothing whatever there. I should never have
eaten that pig's trotter last thing at night,
Carlo. That's what did it.

CARLO: The way you wolfed it down, I'm not surprised.
Anyway...I'm off out.

ALBERTO: Off out? Off out where?

CARLO: I'm meeting someone. In the Piazza Francese.
I shan't be more than an hour or so.

ALBERTO: You don't mean to say you're going out and
leaving me here on my own?

CARLO: Slide the bolt across. I shan't be gone long.

> [CARLO *takes his hat and an umbrella,
> and then hesitates.*]

Wait. I'd better take this instead.

> [*He puts the umbrella back and takes a
> heavy, gnarled walking stick instead.*]

In case I happen to run into one of the
Cimmarutas.

ALBERTO: You'd be better off leaving them both behind.
You're not any too quick off the mark...he'll
simply snatch it out of your hand and clout
you over the head with it.

CARLO: Yes. You may be right.

> [*He puts the stick back.*]

I'll go unarmed. And don't start worrying, Albe.

> [*He goes.* ZI NICOLA *lets off a series of rhythmic bangs from the gallery.*]

ALBERTO: Weren't you listening? We've been talking for the last quarter of an hour. I went to the police station, yes, and they've let me go.

> [*More bangs.*]

No, no. It's not serious. Nothing to get unduly worried about.

> [*More bangs.*]

Of course I won't do anything rash.

> [*The doorbell sounds.*]

Oh, my God...!

> [*He takes the heavy stick* CARLO *has left behind and hides it under his coat before going cautiously out to answer the door.*]

[*off*] Who's there?...Who?...Oh. What's it about, then?...Is there anybody with you?... All right. As long as you're alone. Wait a minute, and I'll let you in.

> [*He comes back in, looking apprehensive, followed by* ROSA, *who is carrying a cup of hot milk.*]

I can't imagine what you can possibly want to see me about.

ROSA: A good neighbour is a blessing sent from God, don Albe. It's partly to do with what happened this morning. You can imagine how we were feeling by the time we got back here from the police station. We were all in. To think of cooking a meal was out of the question, but there was some milk in the house, so I thought the best thing to do was to heat some of that and make us all some coffee. Don Pasquale's lying down at the moment, on his bed, resting. And so is donna Mathilde. So I thought

I'd come across with a cup for you, too. It must have been just as much of an ordeal for you as it was for us, and I don't suppose you've had so much as a glass of water, have you?

ALBERTO: This is very unexpected, donna Rosa. I fully expected you to be furious with me.

ROSA: Furious? It takes great strength of character to do what you did, don Albe. It can't have been easy. A dream like that must leave you absolutely drained. But what is there to say? We must just see how things turn out. One thing, though, I would like to ask you. You can confide in me, don Albe. I've had my share of troubles too...I know what it's like. Are you absolutely certain it was nothing more than a dream you had?

ALBERTO: What are you getting at...?

ROSA: God give me strength to say what I have to say!

ALBERTO: Don't upset yourself, donna Rosa. You can trust me.

ROSA: But can I? Can we trust anyone any more? Don't misunderstand me, but...I don't know, perhaps it's that my nerves are all on edge still from this morning...but there are times...I know it's wicked to talk like this, don Albe... but there are times when I could throw open the window and fling myself out.

[*She breaks down, weeping, and then braces herself.*]

Don Albe...I've only got the one nephew...as you know...Luigino...I'd go to the stake for that boy, don Albe...but somehow he seems to have gone completely off the rails. He talks about wanting to get a job and settle down, but he never finds anything that suits him. I don't know what's wrong with young people

today. They seem to have such a warped out-
look on things...they're so cynical about
everything...they don't believe in anything
any more.

ALBERTO: You can't hold it against them, donna Rosa.
They've grown up in terrible times.

ROSA: He's so full of resentment towards everybody.
Won't listen to anything you say to him. I just
don't understand him. I don't understand his
attitude. When you say it was all nothing
more than a dream...tell me honestly...
between you and me...*was* it?

ALBERTO: I've told you. Yes. I dreamt it.

ROSA: Suppose it was nothing of the kind. Suppose
you're saying you dreamt it because, when it
came to it, you didn't want to produce the
evidence...because you took pity on us and
thought we'd suffered enough. I don't want to
jump to conclusions, don Albe, and only God
Himself knows what it costs me to say this...
and may He strike me down if my heart isn't
breaking...but suppose Aniello Amitrano
was murdered by my nephew?
[*She weeps uncontrollably.*]

ALBERTO: That's a dreadful thing to say, donna Rosa!
Even if you're only half serious.

ROSA: You must know who it was who did it, don
Albe. You've got the papers...they must have
it on them who was responsible. There's
nothing more I can say. But remember what
I've told you...he's the only nephew I have...
Tell them I was the one who did it.

ALBERTO: Donna Rosa...I swear to you it was only a
dream. That's all it was.

ROSA: Yes. I understand. It was all a dream. You'll
have to excuse me, don Albe. I shall have to
go and get something in that I can heat up. I
can't possibly put my mind to cooking with

all this hanging over us. I'll bring something
in for you, too. Something done in batter...
some polenta and a piece or two of fish. A
good neighbour is a blessing sent from God,
don Albe.

> [ROSA *goes out.* ALBERTO *stands there
> lost in thought.* ZI NICOLA *lets off some
> bangs which startle* ALBERTO, *who
> clutches his heart.*]

ALBERTO: It was donna Rosa! Don Pasquale Cimmaruta's sister!

> [*More bangs.*]

A cup of coffee...[*looking into the cup*]...milk...

> [*The doorbell sounds.*]

Now who is it?

> [*He goes out.*]

[*off*] Oh. Come in.

> [*He comes back, followed by* ELVIRA.]

ELVIRA: Has she gone?

ALBERTO: Who?

ELVIRA: My aunt.

ALBERTO: Donna Rosa's gone, yes. She's gone to do
some shopping.

ELVIRA: Can I talk to you? It won't take five minutes.

ALBERTO: Of course you can talk to me. What did you
want to talk to me about?

> [*The doorbell sounds again.*]

I shan't be a moment.

> [*He goes out and comes back almost at
> once.*]

It's your brother.

ELVIRA: My brother? It can't be my brother! He was
supposed to be going out. What's my brother
doing here? Oh, my God!

ALBERTO: What do you want me to do? Send him away?

ELVIRA: No. Let him in. I'll go in there. I didn't tell
anyone I was coming to see you, so he doesn't
know I'm here. Come and tell me when he's
gone.

[ELVIRA *goes out through the door, left, into the apartment, and* ALBERTO *goes out, right, to the hall. He comes back in with* LUIGI.]

ALBERTO: Is there something you wanted to see me about?

LUIGI: Obviously I've got something I want to see you about. What else would I have come here for? That's the sort of question I'd expect someone of your generation to ask. Every time you open your mouths you come out with something stunningly obvious. You're like my parents.

ALBERTO: And how does a boring old fart like me have to phrase things so as to meet with the approval of your vibrant generation?

LUIGI: You say 'Well?'...and put a question mark after it, like that...[*He traces a huge question mark in the air with his finger.*]That's all it needs.

ALBERTO: Well?

[ALBERTO *traces an even more exaggerated question mark in the air.*]

LUIGI: Right. Now listen to what I'm going to say.

ALBERTO: Hold on. I'm anxious to learn. When I said 'Well?...[*Another question mark.*]...it meant I was listening. So why do you say 'Listen to what I'm going to tell you'? It seems superfluous.

LUIGI: [*caught out*] Yes...well...all right. What I came to say.

ALBERTO: But...just a minute...it's obvious you've come to say something...so I can't quite grasp why it's necessary to spell it out...

LUIGI: Look! Are you trying to needle me?

ALBERTO: No, no. Not at all. Far from it. At my age you find it difficult to grasp things.

LUIGI: Well, don't bother. We just don't speak the same language as one another. Just go off somewhere and die...you're just cluttering up the planet.

ALBERTO: True. But so are we all, and, if you can just exercise a little patience, there won't be any of us around at all any more. A clean, uncluttered planet.

LUIGI: I don't know what you're on about, but it doesn't matter because what I've come to tell you is that I know who did it. At least, I have a pretty good idea. It was my aunt.

ALBERTO: Your aunt.

LUIGI: Yes.

ALBERTO: And you come out with it just like that.

LUIGI: How else should I come out with it? She's got this locked room...all right?...and she spends all her time there and won't let anybody else in...and she makes soap in there. Soap and candles. What other proof do you need?

ALBERTO: Are you saying what I think you're saying?

LUIGI: And my sister's mixed up in it as well, because she's the only one who's ever allowed in there.

ALBERTO: Let me get this right. You're saying your aunt murdered Aniello Amitrano in order to turn him into soap...?

LUIGI: And candles.

ALBERTO: What makes you so sure?

LUIGI: What makes you so sure it was only a dream?

ALBERTO: Because there isn't any proof! There are no papers. There's nothing. As God is my witness.

LUIGI: Who are you trying to fool, old man? All a dream! You've just chickened out. You got frightened. So don't try and pull the wool over my eyes. You may fool the police, but you don't fool me. I know who did it, and I've got a houseful of soap and candles to prove it, and you can do what you like about it. Pleasant dreams, grandad.

[LUIGI *goes.* ALBERTO *sits down, abso-*

lutely shattered.]

ALBERTO: My God! [*to* ZI NICOLA] Zi Nicola…how right you are to keep quiet. No one has the slightest self-control any more. They'll come out with anything. [*A pause.*] At the same time…there's no getting away from the fact that I've been keeping watch on their movements. Could I be imagining I dreamt it?

> [*It has begun to get dark.* ALBERTO *goes out and comes back, followed by* PAS-QUALE, *who is carrying a bundle in a black cloth. He is pale and agitated.*]

What have *you* come for?

PASQUALE: I've just taken the opportunity to slip out while my wife's asleep. My son and daughter have both gone out, and my sister's shopping, so it seemed a good moment to come across and have a quiet word with you. It won't take more than a few moments. It's not good to stay locked indoors on your own…things start to go round and round in your mind and, if you're not careful, you can end up talking to yourself, which is the first sign that you're going mad.

ALBERTO: Yes, I understand what it's like.

PASQUALE: I must have someone to unburden myself to, don Albe. I can't go on bottling it up for ever.

ALBERTO: It's always a good thing to share your worries with other people, don Pasquale. A sympathetic ear…it can make all the difference. Confiding in a friend or neighbour…

PASQUALE: People are very quick to stand in judgment, don Albe. They don't always stop to consider what might lie behind outward appearances. That something might have happened in a man's life to make him what he is. When I think back to when I was a child, don Albe, I can hardly recognise myself…then and now.

That little chubby-faced boy…in a sailor suit with a whistle dangling from the pocket on a white cord…yelling for ice-cream outside Pintauro's…can that be the same person I see when I look in the mirror now? Coming home on my sixteenth birthday…proud as punch because I'd passed my book-keeping exam… and announcing to everyone that I was a fully-fledged accountant…! And look at me. Look at the pathetic wreck. Look what I've sunk to. The dregs of humanity. Rock bottom. There isn't anywhere lower I can sink to.

ALBERTO: My dear Pasquale…you mustn't let things get you down like this! Cheer up, man! Look on the bright side.

PASQUALE: I've been a victim of circumstances, don Albe. I'm not rotten through and through. It's life that's done it to me. You wouldn't believe the agonies I've gone through…trying to get to the bottom of what my wife was up to. It's been sheer torment.

ALBERTO: Have you got doubts…?

PASQUALE: When the Blackshirts were around…and then the Germans…we had a secret hiding place made. You got into it through a hole under a sideboard. The whole thing was not much bigger than a rabbit hutch, and every so often my wife would come home with some story that I was wanted for questioning, and I'd have to be bundled into it for my own safety for the night. She kept insisting that I was on their wanted list. So I'd be cooped up in there, terrified out of my wits and hardly daring to breathe, and as a result it's affected my heart so that I haven't been able to work since. Two or three days at a time I'd be stuck in there, and she'd bring me my food. I said 'Who's going to be bothered looking for me?'

It's not as if I'd ever been mixed up in politics. But she'd 'had a phone call'. Someone with a grudge had been talking to the authorities. And all the time I was in there, I was suffering the torments of the damned wondering what she was getting up to behind my back. Then when the war was over...what with my heart condition and being crippled with arthritis... it catches me there when I get it and I'm practically doubled up with pain every time it comes on...I couldn't work and so, to make ends meet, she started reading the cards. She'd done it before, but only as a hobby when we had friends in. Now she was doing it for money. There's a constant stream of clients coming and going...nearly all of them men...and I have to stand outside the door. 'This way, gentlemen. One at a time, please. Madam Omarbey is specially inspired today. Mind the step. Wait your turn.' They're in there with her for over an hour sometimes. An hour! How long does it take to read a few cards? And all the time I'm standing outside the door wondering how much longer they're going to be in there. It's as much as I can do sometimes not to bend down and look through the keyhole. In fact I went so far as to bore a hole...there's a partition with a box-room on the other side...so that I could climb up on a chair and see what was going on in there.

ALBERTO: What did you see?

PASQUALE: I've never been able to pluck up enough courage to look. I no sooner get up on the chair than I think better of it and get down again. But what am I saying all this to you for? You know it all already. You've obviously found out all there is to know about us.

Everything you said this morning confirms
that. But you're wrong if you think I was the
one who did it. Whatever else people may say
about me, don Albe, I've never gone so far as
to murder anyone. At least my hands are
clean on that score. I haven't shed blood.

ALBERTO: Don Pasquale…I'm utterly confused about it
all. Whether it was a dream I had…

PASQUALE: Bring out the evidence, don Albe. Let's have
the culprit…whoever it is…brought to book.
So that he can pay for his crime. Life does
dreadful things to one, don Albe. I wasn't
always the miserable wretch you're looking at
now. There's plenty of good there still if you
dig down deep enough. I haven't broken faith
entirely with the person I was once. I haven't
entirely lost my childhood innocence. [*He
starts to unwrap his bundle.*] Look. Look at this.
This is what I wear on my head when I'm
showing my wife's clients in. I've brought it
with me so that you can see the depths I've
sunk to. [*He takes out a turban.*] Here it is.
Pasquale Cimmaruta's turban. And yet…
even with this on…when I'm standing there
coming out with my patter…'Step this way,
gentlemen. One at a time, please.'…I can still
feel that whistle on the little boy's sailor suit. I
can still taste Pintauro's ice-cream on my
tongue. Here…put it on, Cimmaruta. Let
everyone see what life has brought you to.

> [*He puts the turban on his head, goes to the
> door, and then, turning to face* ALBERTO,
> *draws himself up to his full height, strikes
> a 'heroic' pose, and goes through his patter.*]

There. How do you like it? 'Step this way,
gentlemen, please. Take your turn. One at a
time, gentlemen. Madame Omarbey is
specially inspired today. Step this way.'

[*He breaks down, unable to go on.*]

[*indicating the turban*] This is my badge of shame, don Albe. [*He pulls the turban down over his eyes.*] You're looking at Pasquale Cimmaruta playing blind man's buff.

[*As he feels his way out of the room,* ZI NICOLA *spits on him from the gallery, but he does not notice.*]

MATHILDE: [*off*] So here you are! I knew this was where I'd find you! Playing the idiot with your turban on. You came here for one purpose, didn't you? To spread lies about me behind my back!

[MATHILDE *comes in, beside herself with rage, and dragging* PASQUALE *after her, his turban awry.*]

[*to* ALBERTO] He leaves me to support the family single-handed…dishing out a lot of mumbo-jumbo to cretins all day long to bring some money into the house…and then he has the gall to play the jealous husband, if you please! And the minute I've finished my consultations…on the dot of half past five… where is he? I'll tell you where he is. He's off out. With his cronies. Till four or five o'clock in the morning. And, if you want to know what he's doing, he's throwing his money away gambling. And when it's all gone, he'll stop at nothing to get some more, so he can lose that as well.

PASQUALE: Have you gone completely mad, woman?

MATHILDE: You'd like to think that, wouldn't you? Where were you last night…and the night before… when you didn't come home till morning. Why were you struck suddenly dumb when the Commissioner said we could go because don Alberto had admitted it was all a dream? You went as white as a sheet.

PASQUALE: What are you insinuating?

MATHILDE: I'm insinuating that I think you capable of anything. That's what I'm insinuating.

PASQUALE: And by 'anything', I suppose you mean murdering Aniello Amitrano.

MATHILDE: Yes. If you want to know. That's precisely what I do mean.

PASQUALE: Right. Then I'll ask you something. Where were you last Sunday...when you were out till well after midnight...?

MATHILDE: Never you mind where I was! Where I go is my own business!

PASQUALE: 'Air! Sun!' she said. 'I must be alone!' You're the one who's capable of anything. With your various women friends and all the other riff-raff you hang around with.

MATHILDE: Have you finished?

PASQUALE: Oh, no. Oh, no. I haven't finished. Not by a long way. There are things that have got to be said. Things that have got to come out. Don Alberto has put his finger on a crime. A murder has been committed by a member of this family, and...[*He points accusingly at* MATHILDE.]...and there's only one person it can be...!
      [ELVIRA *comes running in to her mother.*]

ELVIRA: Mummy!
      [ELVIRA *whispers something to* MATHILDE.]

MATHILDE: I don't believe it! I refuse to believe it! Not your brother! Not Luigi! You can't possibly suspect Luigi!

ELVIRA: It was him, Mother! I know it was him!
      [ELVIRA *runs out.* MATHILDE *runs after her.*]

MATHILDE: Elvira! Come back! For pity's sake, Elvira!

PASQUALE: Don Alberto...you've got to listen to me and produce the evidence. Put us out of our agony, don Alberto...put us out of our agony...

> [PASQUALE *goes out after his wife and daughter.* CARLO *enters.*]

CARLO: What's been going on?

ALBERTO: It's no good asking me, Carlo. I know less and less about what's going on. It's beginning to look as if there was a crime after all. They've all been in here one after another accusing someone else of having done it. I tell them there isn't a single shred of evidence, and they just refuse point blank to take any notice.

CARLO: Look, Albe. Once and for all...have you got some evidence, or haven't you?

ALBERTO: I don't know, Carlo. I simply don't know. I could be asleep now, for all I know, dreaming this. Or I could have been awake when I was having what I thought was a dream. One minute I can see all the stuff there perfectly clearly, and the next it's vanished. I don't know what to think. Is the door shut out there?

CARLO: Of course it is.

ALBERTO: Put the bolt across. Don't answer if anyone rings. I want to be left alone to think.

> [*The doorbell sounds.*]

I thought it might be a pious hope!

CARLO: [*calling*] Who is it?

MICHELE: [*off*] It's me...Michele. Let me in.

CARLO: Shall I?

ALBERTO: If it's Michele come back, you'd better.

> [CARLO *goes out and comes back in with* MICHELE.]

MICHELE: Well. I went there.

ALBERTO: And what did you find out?

MICHELE: I'll leave someone else to tell you. [*calling*] You can come in.

> [AMITRANO*'s wife,* TERESA, *enters.*]

This is Aniello Amitrano's wife. Donna Teresa. She wants to talk to you.

[TERESA *goes straight to* ALBERTO.]

TERESA: They've murdered him! They've murdered my husband! He was getting better...he was almost cured...You could see him putting on weight...and now he's dead! There were only two pills left in the bottle...and now he's never going to be able to take them...! My poor Aniello...shall I take them for you, or shall I put them in an urn on the mantelpiece...?

[*She breaks down in tears.*]

It's three days now since he went out of the house, and not a word from him! He's been murdered! He must have been murdered! They've murdered my Aniello! He's been done to death by those butchers in there!

ALBERTO: Sit down, donna Teresa. Try to be calm.

TERESA: I think it's wicked of you not to come forward if you know who did it. People who commit a crime like that should be caught. They should be made to roast in hell. You're no better than they are if you shield them. You're an accomplice!

CARLO: She's right, Albe. You must tell us what you've done with the evidence. There's nothing for it.

ALBERTO: There isn't any evidence! How many times do I have to say it? Do I have to throw myself off the Eiffel Tower before anyone'll listen to what I'm saying? There's no evidence.

TERESA: He said you found Aniello's shirt...and that it was all covered in blood...and one of his shoes.

ALBERTO: [*to* MICHELE] Is that what you told her?

MICHELE: It's what you told me.

TERESA: Surely you can't refuse to let me have his shoe, don Alberto? At least his shoe.

ALBERTO: I don't have his shoe to give you, donna Teresa! If I had his shoe, I'd give you his shoe!

TERESA: Aniello! Aniello! Where are you? Speak to me, Aniello! I knew something like this was going to happen. I had a presentiment. I dreamt all my teeth fell out. Aniello! What have they done to you? What have those ruffians done to you, Aniello? My poor Aniello!

[ZI NICOLA *comes out from behind his curtain and leans over the rail of the gallery. He speaks in a clear voice, pronouncing each word very precisely.*]

ZI NICOLA: Could we have a fraction less noise down there, please?

[*He goes back behind the curtain.*]

CARLO: Did you hear that? He spoke! Zi Nicola spoke!

ALBERTO: He's finally broken his vow.

[*A brilliant green light is to be seen coming from the gallery.*]

CARLO: Zi Nico…Zi Nico…

ALBERTO: That was the Roman candle.

CARLO: Zi Nico…Zi Nico…

[ZI NICOLA *lifts a corner of the curtain and puts the roman candle into a metal tube which has been fixed to the rail of the gallery for the purpose. He drops the curtain.* CARLO *goes up the ladder to the gallery.*]

Zi Nico…what's wrong, Zi Nico? What's the matter?…Zi Nico. Answer me. Zi Nico…[*He calls down.*] He's dead, Albe. Zi Nicola's dead.

ALBERTO: I can't believe that.

CARLO: He is, Albe. Come up.

ALBERTO: You're letting your imagination run away

with you, Carlo. I couldn't face it if Zi Nicola were dead.

MICHELE: Poor Zi Nicola. I'm sorry if he's gone. I shall miss him.

CARLO: What a beautiful face he has, Albe. He looks like a saint lying here.

[*It is now almost dark in the room.*]

Switch the light on, Albe.

MICHELE: It's no good. The electricity's off. They're doing something to the mains. No one in the building's got any light till it comes back on.

[ALBERTO *tries the switch, but nothing happens.*]

ALBERTO: If it's not one thing, it's something else.

[TERESA *is quietly moaning to herself.*]

TERESA: What have they done to you, Aniello? I should never have let you go. Oh, my poor Aniello.

ROSA: [*off*] May I come in?

[ROSA *enters.*]

ALBERTO: [*to* MICHELE] You didn't shut the front door.

ROSA: A good neighbour is a blessing sent from God, don Albe. [*calling*] Come in, Maria.

[MARIA *comes in carrying a candelabra with five lighted candles on it. She hands it to* ROSA, *who walks to the table with it and sets it down. They are her own candles, and she is visibly pleased with them.*]

Thanks be to God, don Albe, that we have these. Don't they give a lovely light!

[ROSA *goes out with* MARIA. TERESA *continues moaning.* ALBERTO, *remembering* LUIGI's *accusations, looks at the candles in horror. He glances across at* TERESA, *and then back at the candles.*]

ACT THREE

The following morning. Nothing has changed except that ZI NICOLA *is no longer up in the gallery, and the curtains have been taken down and piled up on one side so that all his private possessions are exposed to view.*

ALBERTO *is pacing up and down in a state of agitation and stopping every so often to speak to* MICHELE, *who is standing by the door, right.*

ALBERTO: When I see what the human race is capable of, I'm ashamed to be part of it.

MICHELE: I only told you so that you'd know what was going on. I thought it might put you on your guard.

ALBERTO: I'd sooner be an ape than a human being. I'd sooner be a parrot. A parrot comes out with a lot of rubbish, but you can't blame the parrot because a parrot doesn't have the faintest idea what it's talking about.

MICHELE: You're saying things that I've often thought myself, don Alberto, but I've never been able to put them into words.

ALBERTO: We're witnessing the last judgment, Michele, if we did but realise it. You're sure you actually heard all this yourself...

MICHELE: With my own ears. May God make them rot and fall off if I'm telling a lie, don Alberto.

ALBERTO: The depths to which people can sink...!

MICHELE: They were together for more than an hour and a half...that was yesterday. And then this morning they were talking just outside the door, and I was in my cubbyhole down there so I could hear everything they were saying. Your brother was telling the other man that he'd seen the lieutenant, and had had it from his own lips that they were going to come and arrest you, and then he said 'Once he's out of the house, we can load the whole lot straight on to the handcart and we can clinch the deal.' Those were near enough his words.

ALBERTO: Would you have believed it? Would you have believed that your own brother would be capable of it? To wait till you were taken off to prison, and then strip you of every miserable rag you've got to your name.

MICHELE: Ties of blood count for nothing when money comes into it, don Alberto. It's the law of the jungle. It doesn't surprise me where your brother's concerned. I don't mean to give offence, but your brother isn't at all popular in the way you are. You're popularity itself, but your brother antagonises people. He has too high an opinion of himself. It puts people's backs up. 'Don Alberto's all right,' people say, 'but his brother...' And all that time he spends in church. There's nothing wrong with being pious...it's a good thing... but you can carry it too far.

ALBERTO: The reason he's never out of church is that he can't wait to go to confession and get what he's done off his chest ready to start all over again with a clean slate. This time he's over-reached himself. I shall wait till I've found out what it is he's up to, and then I'll know how to deal with it.

MICHELE: Don't forget I've said nothing. It's between you and your brother. I don't want my name brought into it. I'm just telling you what I overheard.

[*He starts to go, then comes back.*]

What I came up here for was to ask whether you want me to have a wreath put downstairs outside the main door for...

> [*He gestures up to* ZI NICOLA*'s gallery.*]

ALBERTO: Of course I want a wreath! It's not someone's budgerigar that's dropped dead!

MICHELE: [*crosses himself*] What a thing to say, don Alberto! No...the thought that crossed my mind was that as he was taken away in an ambulance and died at the hospital...

ALBERTO: He may have died at the hospital, but he lived here!

MICHELE: Yes. The thing is...young de Ferraris's mother...she's got a bad heart and he's afraid if she happens to catch sight of a wreath standing outside...there's no knowing how it might affect her. So I was wondering what to do for the best.

ALBERTO: Forget it.

MICHELE: I know Zi Nicola wouldn't have cared one way or the other. He never had much time for ceremony.

ALBERTO: It's true. He didn't. He was above all that kind of thing. I'm only just beginning to appreciate what a splendid man he was. He was far wiser than he seemed. He must have suffered a lot of hardship through refusing to talk. I think I'll go and put a carnation on his coffin.

MICHELE: He wouldn't want it, don Alberto. Zi Nicola was never one for flowers. Good deeds and fireworks were what he was interested in. But...I'll be off.

> [MICHELE *goes out. There is an urgent re-peated knocking at the door, left.* ALBERTO *starts to cross towards it when the doorbell sounds.*]

ALBERTO: Not yet! You'll have to wait. Just give me ten minutes, and I'll be with you.

> [ALBERTO *goes out, right, and comes back*

in with MARIA. *She is carrying an old battered suitcase which is tied with string and bursting open. She has various other parcels and bundles.*]

What's happened, Maria? What's it all about?

MARIA: I'll tell you, don Alberto. Is the door shut?

ALBERTO: Yes. What are you doing with all this?

MARIA: I'm going. I wouldn't stay on in a house with people like that. If they hadn't given me notice, I was going to give them notice.

ALBERTO: Tell me what all this is about, Maria.

MARIA: I must sit down, don Alberto. I hardly slept last night. [*She sits.*] I'm not fit for anything if I don't get a proper night's sleep. It's the way I'm made. My body needs more sleep than other people's.

ALBERTO: So what have you come to tell me?

MARIA: You must get away from here, don Alberto. You must pack now and go, before it's too late. You just don't know what these people are like. They're monsters. I'll tell you everything I can, but don't whatever you do bring my name into it, or they'll have me strangled. They're quite capable of it. They'll come to my village looking for me, and they'll drag me out of bed and kill me if they think I've been talking.

ALBERTO: Talking about what?

MARIA: Well...you're not going to believe this...but you remember yesterday evening...when the electricity was cut off and donna Rosa came in here with her candles...

ALBERTO: Am I likely to forget it?

MARIA: Well...later on I was in my room...and it was all still in darkness...and I could hear voices raised. I was wondering what it was all about, and then suddenly pandemonium broke out.

They were all yelling and shouting at one another. 'It was you!' '...No, it wasn't! It was you!' And then I heard don Pasquale slap his wife across the face, Elvira fainted and had to be brought round, and donna Rosa was in tears...it was absolute bedlam. And it went on for two solid hours. Then it suddenly all went quiet and I could hear them crying and trying to make it up with one another. Then one of them...don Pasquale it was...said 'It's no use. One of us has got to own up. Don Alberto's got the evidence.' Then it went quiet again and I couldn't hear anything more, but after a time there was a tap on my bedroom door and it was donna Mathilde. She said 'You must go, Maria. Get up and pack your things and go.' I said 'But I've got nowhere to go. Where can I possibly go to at this time?' She said 'That's up to you. You'll have to find somewhere. But you must get out at once.' So I said 'Well, all right, then. I'll leave first thing in the morning.' She said 'No, you must go now. It's still quite early. There's plenty of time to look for somewhere else.' I said 'Look for another job at this time? You can't be serious, donna Mathilde!' She said 'It's only six o'clock. You've got three hours yet before your bedtime.' So I thought to myself 'There's something funny going on here', so I said 'All right. If that's what you want, I'll take my things off and go now.' So I let her go out of the room and left it for a minute or two, and then I went down and opened the front door and then shut it again as loud as I could so as to make them think I'd gone, and then I tiptoed back to my room and listened at the door.

ALBERTO: And what did you hear?

MARIA: .Well…I couldn't make out everything they were saying…but from the bits I heard they're planning to kill you. They think it's their only hope. They think, if you're out of the way, and you haven't told anybody where the evidence is hidden, they'll be in the clear.

ALBERTO: [*unruffled*] I see. And was this all in so many words?

MARIA: I had to piece it together, but yes. The idea is to come here and invite you to go on a picnic with them in the country somewhere. And once they've got you there…and there's no one else about…they can do whatever they like and who's to know?

ALBERTO: Who, indeed?

MARIA: They were serious. I could hear them discussing it. Don Pasquale was all for taking you on a stroll by yourself after lunch in order to get you alone. I didn't tumble at first, then Luigi said 'No. Don't do that. We'll take him on a boat trip instead. And then, when we're far enough out…' But donna Rosa said 'No. Leave it to me.' What else could it mean? They're going to kill you, don Alberto.

ALBERTO: Possibly. Or it could simply be that they want to try and talk me into handing over the evidence.

MARIA: But why would they want me out of the way? What was all the whispering for? Why would they want to take you out in a boat?

ALBERTO: I don't think they're likely to do anything very desperate.

MARIA: You weren't there! You didn't hear them talking!

ALBERTO: It's not of any great importance. I'm not going to let it worry me. If they want to come and invite me to go on a picnic with them, I shall be very happy to accompany them. It might be quite enjoyable.

MARIA: It'd be madness, don Alberto! You can't possibly go! You've got to get away from here. While there's still time. Or else hand the evidence over to the police, so that they can all be arrested. That's if there really is any evidence.

ALBERTO: Oh, yes. There's evidence. Any amount of evidence.

MARIA: Well, then, why don't you do something? What are you waiting for?

ALBERTO: I'm waiting to be asked to go on a picnic.

MARIA: All right...but don't say I didn't warn you. I've done everything I can. If something happens, it won't be on my conscience.

ALBERTO: No. You did the right thing, Maria.

[ALBERTO *suddenly buries his face in his hands*.]

Good God! What a world! What a place for a young girl to have grown up in! So what are you planning to do now?

MARIA: I haven't thought, really. I could go back home, except that they wouldn't exactly be overjoyed at having another mouth to feed. The only thing I can think of is to see if they can find me anything down at the agency, then I can stay on here with some other family.

ALBERTO: It's an odd business, isn't it, when you come to think of it. You go into a completely strange house amongst a lot of people you don't know, and with no idea what's in store for you when you get there – and they're just as much in the dark about you...and there it is. You must go. Good luck, and God bless you.

MARIA: But you're not going to stay here! Aren't you going to make a dash for it while you can?

ALBERTO: No, Maria. There's the evidence. All the

evidence that's required, anyway.

MARIA: Well...I've done my best to warn you. Good luck is all I can say.

[*She gathers up her things and starts to go.*]

The one I really had it in for there was donna Rosa. That old bitch used to make me get out of bed as soon as it was light every morning... and I need my sleep...

ALBERTO: Leave the door open. It'll save them the trouble of ringing the bell when they come about the picnic.

MARIA: My word...you're the coolest person I've ever known! I think that shows real courage! I admire someone like that.

[*She goes.* ALBERTO *sits thinking for a moment, and then goes out through the door, left.*]

ALBERTO: Yes. All right. It's me. I'm coming.

[PASQUALE *enters, calm and relaxed, from the right. He is wearing a new suit, and has a flower in his buttonhole. His right hand is bandaged.*]

PASQUALE: No one here? Don Albe! Where are you?

[ALBERTO *comes back.*]

ALBERTO: Don Pasquale. My, my. You're looking very spruce this morning.

PASQUALE: Oh...do you think so? It's just a gesture, really. I thought it might bring about a change of luck to wear something different. We had a bit of a set-to last night. We let ourselves go rather. Look at that. See the way it's swollen up. [*He shows* ALBERTO *his bandaged hand.*] That was from thumping the table. You don't notice you're doing it at the time. But, then, once we'd let off steam and began to calm down, we looked at the thing again in a more balanced frame of mind and came to

the conclusion that there was nothing more to
it, when you came down to it, than that
wretched dream of yours.

ALBERTO: So you've finally come round to it that it was
nothing more than a dream.

PASQUALE: We did eventually…but we were all a bit
overwrought…a trying day, and…you know
how it is…you keep going over and over the
same thing until you get to the point where
you can't tell what makes sense and what
doesn't. So this morning I said to the family
'Look…it's a nice day…why don't we all get
dressed up and go off for a picnic somewhere…?' My sister never gets out…it would
do her good.

ALBERTO: Most sensible thing you could have done. It's
a lovely day for it.

PASQUALE: [*gesturing up to the gallery*] How is…?

ALBERTO: Zi Nicola? He's no longer with us.

PASQUALE: I know, but…

ALBERTO: He was taken to the hospital when the doctor
couldn't do anything, and he died there in the
night.

PASQUALE: Such a good man. A saint, almost, in his own
way.

ALBERTO: I'm only now beginning to realise just how
much of a saint he was. Eighty-two…!

PASQUALE: Those fireworks…

ALBERTO: No one else could understand him but me. He
wouldn't bother letting them off for anybody
else. Poor Zi Nicola. He was one in a million.

PASQUALE: Don Albe…a thought's just struck me.
Instead of staying here…why not come with
us? It'd do you good to get out. We were
thinking of going to Pozzuoli…or somewhere
in that direction…Bacoli, perhaps…it's very
mild out…it really is…and then, after we've
had some lunch, we could perhaps go out for a

boat ride, the two of us. I heard a story the other day that I've been wanting to tell you... it made me laugh so much the tears were running down my face...so why don't we all meet on the corner down by San Pasquale and then we can go off together? That way no one's going to see us and start passing comments. You know what people are... 'There he goes...his uncle only just dead, and he's off out with his friends enjoying himself.'

ALBERTO: Oh, yes. I know how people's minds work.

PASQUALE: What do you say? Will you come?

ALBERTO: Well...it's very kind. The last thing I expected was to be invited to go on a picnic. Yes...I'd be delighted. I'll come as I am. I won't dress up specially.

PASQUALE: Come just as you like.

> [ROSA *enters, followed by the rest of the family, all dressed up for the occasion and eager to get started.*]

LUIGI: Well...what's the hold-up, then?

ROSA: We're all ready.

MATHILDE: It's a lovely day...it couldn't be more perfect for it...

ELVIRA: I can't wait for us to get started.

LUIGI: I'm taking Aunt Rosa. We'll go off arm in arm, won't we, Aunt Rosa?

ROSA: People'll think we're sweethearts.

PASQUALE: I've got some news for you. Don Alberto's coming with us.

ALL: Oh, well...that makes it absolutely perfect... Lovely!...Hooray!...[*etc.*]

LUIGI: I'll take don Alberto's arm in that case!

PASQUALE: We all will. We'll take turns. Are we ready to go, then? [*to* ALBERTO] Don't let on to anyone that you're coming with us, will you?

ALBERTO: No, no.

PASQUALE: It doesn't matter to us, but it might be better

from your point of view. If I were you, I shouldn't even mention it to don Carlo.

ALBERTO: I'll just say I've gone out for a stroll on my own. To try and get one or two things sorted out in my mind.

PASQUALE: That's it. We'll be waiting at the corner for you, and then we can all go off together. But don't start having second thoughts, will you, the moment we've left.

ALBERTO: No fear of that. Ten minutes, and I'll be with you.

LUIGI: If you haven't turned up in a quarter of an hour, I'm coming straight back here to fetch you.

ALBERTO: You won't have to do that.

[*They are all about to leave when* CARLO *enters followed by* CAPA D'ANGELO.]

CARLO: What's happening here? It looks like a party.

PASQUALE: We're off out for the day...we thought we'd have a picnic.

ALBERTO: They've just looked in to say goodbye before they go.

CARLO: You couldn't have chosen a better day for it.

ALBERTO: I'm going out for a stroll myself in a minute or two. I want to get some air and think things over.

CARLO: Yes, that's a good idea. I should do that.

[ALBERTO *turns to* CAPA D'ANGELO.]

ALBERTO: Who would this be?

CARLO: Oh, yes...this is a friend of mine. He's had a bit of a misunderstanding with his fiancée... haven't you?...and they're not on speaking terms, so I thought...until it blows over...he could stay here rather than run the risk of their running into one another in the street. He's been through it a bit, one way and another, so I don't want to go out and leave him here on his own. As soon as he's feeling

more himself, and there's no sign of his fiancée
in the vicinity, he can venture out again.

CAPA: That's right. Venture out.

LUIGI: Well...are we going to get started, then?

> [*As they start to leave for the second time,
> the* LIEUTENANT *comes in, followed by*
> MICHELE.]

LIEUTENANT: Well, don Alberto...this looks like it. Aniello
Amitrano is missing from home, and we are
unable to trace his whereabouts, so I've got
no option but to ask you to come with me.

ALBERTO: A warrant for my arrest.

LIEUTENANT: If you want to put it formally, yes.

> [ALBERTO *turns to* CARLO.]

ALBERTO: Well, Carlo...this seems like the moment to
sign that piece of paper of yours.

CARLO: Paper?...Oh, the paper...Yes...[*He starts to
search his pockets.*] I'm not sure if I've still got
it...[*He brings out a piece of paper.*] What's this...?
Yes, here it is...[*He hands it to* AL-
BERTO.]...What a thing to happen!

> [ALBERTO *signs it and hands it back to*
> CARLO.]

ALBERTO: It's in your hands now, Carlo.

CARLO: You can rely on me, Albe. I'll do everything
exactly as you'd have liked it done if you'd
been here to see to it in person.

ALBERTO: You've come at the right moment, lieutenant,
if you hadn't come to see me, I was coming
down to see you.

LIEUTENANT: For what reason?

ALBERTO: I think I've found the evidence we were all
looking for.

LIEUTENANT: Not before time. Where is it?

ALBERTO: You'd like me to produce it now?

LIEUTENANT: Yes. The sooner the better.

ALBERTO: Good. I was hoping you'd say that. One
moment.

[*He goes to the door, left, opens it and calls through.*]

All right. You can come in now.

[TERESA AMITRANO *enters. She is followed by* ANIELLO, *trying unsuccessfully to merge with the background.*]

Let me introduce you. Teresa Amitrano.

TERESA: Hallo.

[*Silence.*]

LIEUTENANT: [*to* ANIELLO] Who are you?

ANIELLO: Aniello Amitrano.

LIEUTENANT: What proof do we have of that?

ANIELLO: Here's my identity card. If that's any use…

[LIEUTENANT *examines it and hands it back.*]

LIEUTENANT: [*accusingly*] You realise you've been the subject of a murder enquiry…

ANIELLO: Yes. I've been told.

TERESA: He's been staying with his aunt…haven't you?

ANIELLO: In Caserta.

TERESA: And then he was taken ill.

ANIELLO: I said 'There's no point in telling my wife. She'll only worry.'

TERESA: And that was why I got worried. We'd had a row…hadn't we?…and when we've had rows before he's often gone off and not come back for two or three days…haven't you?…

ANIELLO: Longer.

TERESA: Longer.

ANIELLO: She wouldn't have thought twice about it if it hadn't been for the porter coming and saying something about a crime.

TERESA: That was what made me think something must have happened to him.

LIEUTENANT: It looks as though that clears that up, then. [*to* ALBERTO] You'll have to come down to police headquarters…there'll be some formalities to attend to…[*to* ANIELLO] and you'd better come as well…but otherwise…unless there are any objections…I think the best thing we can do is to call the incident closed and forget it ever happened.

MATHILDE: Forget it happened! After what we've been through! We've been called murderers, we've been called criminals, we've been dragged down to police headquarters. And now we're supposed to call the incident closed and forget it ever happened!

PASQUALE: Albe…?

ALBERTO: Yes. I did call you murderers. And so you are. We all are, if we did but know it. It's only now beginning to come home to me what sort of crime it is we have all perpetrated on one another. We're doing it all the time but it's become so much second nature to us that we don't notice it any more. I've been waiting for this moment to try and put it into words. And I will. There's just one thing I have to do first. It won't take a moment.

> [ALBERTO *crosses to where* CARLO *is standing and without warning gives him a stinging blow across the face.*]

If you're wondering what that's for, I'll explain another time.

> [CARLO *slowly brings out the piece of paper* ALBERTO *has signed, and hands it back to him.*]

This isn't going to be needed any longer.

> [*He tears the paper into small pieces, and then turns to* CAPA D'ANGELO.]

Goodbye, Capa d'Angelo. I'm afraid there's nothing more we can do for you here. It's quite safe for you to venture out. There's no possibility of running into your fiancée.

CAPA: No. I'll…I'll be going…

ALBERTO: How can I explain? How can I put it into words? What we've killed, between us, is not Aniello here...it's our faith in one another. We've come to the point where any enormity can seem commonplace...something any one of us might easily have been guilty of...and then shifting the blame...wife husband, aunt nephew, sister brother...what sort of a state have we got ourselves into...how can things have come to such a pass...? Words, words, words. You had the right idea, Zi Nicola. You realised how futile words are. You gave up speaking altogether in the end. You were wise enough to realise what I'm only just coming to see. Give me some advice, Zi Nicola. Tell me what to do.

[*There is a sound from outside like a car backfiring in the distance.*]

I didn't catch, Zi Nicola! You'll have to speak more clearly. I can't...

[*Silence.*]

Did you hear?

[*They think it best not to encourage the fantasy.*]

LUIGI: Hear what?

ALBERTO: The fireworks. Didn't you hear them? As if they were a long way away.

ALL: No. I heard nothing. Did you? [*etc.*]

ALBERTO: He was trying to tell me something, but I couldn't make out what it was. I just couldn't get the drift. [*to* LIEUTENANT] Lieutenant...may I have your permission to put off this visit to police headquarters for an hour or two? I feel desperately tired. I think I need to rest.

LIEUTENANT: I'll come back this afternoon.

ALBERTO: Thank you.

PASQUALE: Come on. All the excitement...and his uncle

dying...it's been a bit too much for him. We'll go and leave him in peace to get over it.

> [*They go out, chatting amiably.* ALBERTO, CARLO *and* MICHELE *remain.*]

MICHELE: I never seem to have dreams myself these days. I just fall into bed at the end of the day, and that's it. I'm too tired to sleep sometimes, let alone dream. I had them when I was younger. When I was a boy I had some wonderful dreams. But things were different then. It's all changed now. What with the war, and then the occupation. And the Blackshirts before that. It's surprising anyone trusts anyone any more. Lies, rumours... but I can't stay talking...I've got too much to do. There's only me looking after the whole building.

> [*He starts to go, and then remembers something.*]

Oh...by the way...I put a wreath down there...de Ferraris said his mother's not going out today...she's feeling poorly. I thought it was only right. It's a mark of respect for...[*He nods towards where* ZI NICOLA *used to be.*] Anyway...if you'll excuse me...

> [MICHELE *goes out.* ALBERTO *and* CARLO *are now alone.* ALBERTO *has his head on his arms.* CARLO *is sitting drooped on a chair. After a short pause,* ALBERTO *slowly turns his head and looks at his brother for several moments. He seems on the verge of tears, and then, as if in despair, presses his hands against his face.*]

> [*There is a sudden shaft of sunlight through the dirty panes of the large window high up.*]

THE END